MW01115233

"When you go to Joytown, take two hearts because you will leave one there."

– Mercy Muthumbi Ng'ang'a

Chaplain, Bethany Kids at Kijabe Hospital

take two hearts

One Surgeon's Passion for Disabled Children in Africa

Dr. Richard S. Bransford

with Diane Coleman

Preface

I didn't "take two hearts" into the adventure in 1982. While I was a happy general surgeon, I was unknowingly embarking upon the path of a pioneer. When I visited the pre-school room in Kajiado, I was shocked. Those minutes in that room, observing crutches on the floor and braces on the legs of young Maasai children were vividly etched into my memory, and remain even to this day.

My life was changed, but I had no idea of the great rewards and the heartaches that awaited me. Lest the negative be accentuated too much, I would quickly say that I would retrace my steps without hesitancy, i.e. I would do it all over again. I am so very thankful for the many ways that God has blessed in the years since that visit. Yes, there were heartaches and disappointments, but they in no way compare to the blessings that have come my way.

Twenty-nine years after that visit to Kajiado I left Kijabe and returned to semi-retirement in the U.S. Medically, when I left Africa, BethanyKids at Kijabe Hospital and the Cure International Children's Hospital were in the hands of specialists with skills far beyond my limited abilities. I rejoice in this. But I still dream of a far more extensive network of facilities and staff distributed over more of Africa.

I had, and continue to have, an imagined cadre of workers who, though not well-trained specialists in the wider sense, could be reasonably prepared in a limited period of time to perform a select number of procedures (probably 8-10) on the

< *Kajiado Child Care Center, 1982*

disabled to meet 80-85% of the surgical needs of the disabled. It is my opinion that such a labor force will be necessary in Africa for the next 50-100 years if any reasonable care is to be provided during that time. I also believe that medical care for the disabled cannot wait for those who will be trained in the Western model, and will need to come from a training model

that is not yet "on the table." This will likely be unique for the developing world, or at least that part that can accept something less than "state-of-the-art."

Africa has over one billion people. This suggests that there are 30-100 million disabled people in Africa. Some say that around 20% of these could have their quality of life improved with surgical care. Probably not more than 15% of those needing surgical care can access that care. So, there is a huge task before us.

How do we approach that task optimistically? Medically, there is the potential of vastly improving the quantity and quality of care for the disabled in Africa. Spiritually, Mercy, the BK chaplain, along with the BK staff, and Mercy's team of more than 500 volunteer "disciplers" saw over 37,000 people come to the Lord in a 10-year period. Jesus told his disciples, 'The harvest is plentiful, but the laborers are few; therefore pray earnestly to the Lord of the harvest to send out laborers into his harvest" (Matthew 9: 37, 38). His children have a commission. We are His ambassadors. No one said that it had to be easy, or safe.

What a privilege to be a part of God's plan. I am thankful that I have been able to see a bit of His program in the making, and to participate in helping make at least a part of what I will assume to be His dream come true.

FOREWORD

Dr. Dick Bransford and his wife Millie have been our heroes since we landed in East Africa over 32 years ago. Within the mission community, the Bransford name was known everywhere we traveled. They were held up to us as the epitome of what it meant to be a family on mission with Jesus. Early in their lives, both Dick and Millie had determined to obey Jesus's command to take the Good News wherever Jesus commanded. Obedience to God was the foundation of their relationship.

Take Two Hearts has been one of the hardest books I have ever read. This might sound strange to those who have never given their hearts away. Like the Bransford family, my family and I have had the joy of going with Jesus to some of the most joy-filled places on the planet. Also, like the Bransford family, our obedience to the Great Commission of Jesus Christ has led us to some of the darkest and most dangerous places on the planet. Like the Bransford family, it was important for us to take "two hearts" to Africa so that we could leave one behind wherever we had the joy to serve.

In *Take Two Hearts* one hears the laughter of Africa's children. In its pages you can hear the thump-thump of the generator running the one light in the clinic at night where you are trying to change one more life. You smell the sweat on the bodies of those who have walked endless miles in order to bring their sick or handicapped child to the only doctor they will ever meet. The dust of Africa invades your clothes and your soul to the extent that it becomes part of your inner being. In these stories you can feel your heart race as the pilot of your small plane falls unconscious in the middle the flight! You witness the commitment of an entire family where a father takes his daughters into places of danger because the family has answered the most important question of life, "is Jesus worth it?" with a resounding "Yes." Families do take risks for the sake of the kingdom of God. Dick would say that risks are also taken for the sake of Africa's precious disabled children.

Bransford's love gives Africa and Africans a name. Countries and cities are called by their name as they continue to be a part of God's story. Handicapped children such as Nashurua, Kevin, and Sala are named and become children you want to hold, take home and adopt – much like other children who became part, lovingly and legally, of the Bransford family. Because of their desire to both serve and love who they found inside the borders of Africa's countries, thousands of children have been held, loved and healed. Through this book you get to travel to exotic places like Sudan, Somalia, the Congo, and Kenya – naming just a few of the countries where Dick and his family are still making an eternal difference.

Kijabe Hospital became a part of our personal story, and our growing love for Dick and his family, as we served for seven years in Somalia and its surrounding borders. One particular day is etched in my memory when Al Crow, a retired NFL professional football player, picked up a young boy, crippled by polio. He found this child crawling in the dirt, with his legs dragging behind him, in Mandera, a small town near the border between Kenya and Somalia. I watched this gentle giant cradle this young boy in his arms. Squeezing himself onto a small airplane, he held the child all the way from the border of Somalia to Nairobi, Kenya. Cramped and sweaty, I watched him unfold himself from the small plane, never letting go of the child, as he got into our 4x4 vehicle. From there we drove straight to Kijabe Hospital where Al placed this boy into the competent and caring arms of Dick Bransford. In the care of Dick and his team, this young boy's legs were straightened, and another life was changed. Never again would this child have to crawl in the desert's dirt and dust. Now, today, he walks as a man, married with his own family, standing tall as he herds his camels because of the gifted hands and obedient hearts of men like Al Crow and Dick Bransford.

It is my prayer that God uses *Take Two Hearts* to call another generation of young men and women to obedience. Why should those of us who live in the West have access to doctors of every specialty when millions of the children of Africa will live their entire lives without meeting a medical professional? Yes, riches can be found in bank accounts and retirement funds. But greater are the riches that are found in the smiles of children who can walk, fill their bellies each day with food, and grow up without war being the common environment. Children do not have to crawl in the dust with twisted limbs, go to bed hungry, nor fear the man with the AK-47. *Take Two Hearts* is a book about changing our world. It's a book about obedience to the command of Jesus. It's a book about being family to the families of the world. It's a book about being so loved by God that one cannot keep it to oneself. We have received a gift that must be given away.

Dick Bransford has not done me a favor by allowing me to read his book. Why? Because I would love to start over once more and live another life among the peoples of this earth. I would love to see Africa again for the first time. I would love to hear the laughter of her children, her harmony as she sings, and witness the endless possibilities of this great continent. We would love to watch our children grow up again as we serve Christ together as a family in Africa. May God use Dick's book to open the eyes of thousands of readers who once again will hear the command of Jesus to "go." Go and heal. Go and feed. Go and love. Go and serve. Go and learn from Africa's wisdom, generosity, and graciousness.

Dr. Nik Ripken

Global Strategist, International Mission Board

Author of *The Insanity of God* and *The Insanity of Obedience*

ACKNOWLEDGMENTS

While many of the stories included in this book were writ-ten over a long period of time, nearly all focused upon "my kids." Those children, both living and dead, deserve my heartfelt thanks. Thanks for enthralling me with your needs to such an extent that it has changed my life – for the better. Thanks for sharing yourselves with me in so many ways. Thanks for inviting me to fall in love with a group of children and their parents to whom I would not normally have been attracted.

Thanks to Diane Coleman who helped me compose and complete a task that has been a burden to my soul for a num-ber of years. The "burden" is the need to share this story with a wider audience than just my immediate friends and family. The plight of the disabled in Africa in general is an untold story. In many ways it is the "shame" that has been hidden in the closets of many homes, like so many disabled children. If the "shame" can be exposed, the closet can be opened, and it is more likely the wound will be healed.

Dr. Bill Barnett, my chief mentor and friend, regularly encouraged me to share about the work with the disabled. Jim Taylor, from the time when I was in medical school, was a faithful friend. He is the founder of the International Rehabilitation Mission, Inc. He sought tirelessly to help advance my work with the disabled in Africa.

Drs. Jim Wade, Ivan Stewart and Dan Poenaru labored greatly with the board and the work of BethanyKids. Scott Taylor was also on the BK board and is an unusual visionary. Scott introduced me to Joe Schmidt, founder of the Audacity Factory, and they are continuing to help develop an improved "business plan" for meeting the needs of more disabled children. Brett Margaron and Donald Davis, both former Development Directors for BK, were companions and good friends, and they both built healthy friendships with many of those who believed in BK.

In one way or another each of the above individuals has encouraged these "musings." I am certain that each has a passion to improve the care for the disabled.

Thanks to two young lady doctors in an "unidentified country" who helped share this load for the last nine years. They learned the procedures well enough to effectively meet the needs of many of the disabled in their area of the world. This, to me, demonstrates that these skills can be effectively transferred to others in the developing world. After all, medical workers like these are the future caretakers of the disabled of their area of Africa.

Thanks too to Millie, my wife, for patiently reading, and re-reading, and revising portions of what Diane and I have written. She has been a patient and encouraging companion in this venture and throughout life. I was the evolving "doctor" who eventually would find myself before both medical and spiritual audiences. I would be the one receiving the awards and in the limelight. She, the mother of our children, the hostess, the teacher, and my wife, was the glue that held it all together.

While this has taken time from my family life, hopefully this endeavor will help add years to the lives of many disabled children.

And, immense thanks be to God for His wonderful provision in all that has occurred.

RICHARD BRANSFORD

DAISY

Kijabe, Kenya.

December, 2008

I could make it down the path from our home to the hospital in about one minute in a run, but seldom did I have to make that run anymore. In the "olden days" I took surgical call for anything. Most of those runs were for emergency C-sections. When the call came in the early morning, I enjoyed the blush of dawn coming over the Escarpment, the rim of the Great Rift Valley, as I hastily washed at the scrub sink. After finishing those operations I often returned to the sink to rinse my hands, fantasizing that there was a Denny's Restaurant right across from the hospital. I imagined going there to spend a leisurely hour before rounds, drinking coffee, maybe enjoying an egg and toast, or some other favorite breakfast concoction that wasn't available in Kijabe. I imagined a devotional time in a cozy nook, just dreaming and thinking.

Today is different. I now care for disabled children and the days of frequent emergencies have passed.

Our family had just returned from a week on Diani Beach, south of Mombasa. It was a few days after Christmas and I had been asked to see Daisy. Daisy had been born on January 23, 1999, the first-born of her parents, and had spina bifida (a birth defect where there is incomplete closure of the backbone) and hydrocephalus (a condition that occurs when fluid builds up in the skull and causes the brain to swell). Her first operations, spina bifida closure and initial shunt (a

17

device with a one-way valve that channels brain fluid to the peritoneum where it can be reabsorbed), had been done at the main government hospital in Nairobi when she was just a few months old. When she was three or four she couldn't walk. One day she said to her grandmother, "Grandma, I want to walk!" They prayed together, and Daisy began to walk, though in a halting way.

Daisy had another shunt inserted at BKKH two months before I saw her. Her mother and dad were both nurses in a government hospital about three hours north of Kijabe. When Daisy developed a fever and lethargy, she was treated for malaria. But she did not improve – instead she got worse. She developed a progressive weakness of her left arm and leg until she was essentially paralyzed.

Realizing that Daisy was not improving and the diagnosis of malaria might not be correct, her mother Emma called Agnes Jeruto, one of our rehab nurses. They were asked to bring Daisy to Kijabe Hospital. On their way they passed through Nakuru, where Daisy had a CT scan. This revealed a collection of fluid on the surface of both sides of the brain.

I examined Daisy, heard the history from her mother, checked out the lab tests, and looked at her CT. I explained very carefully to her mother that surgery would likely not lead to full recovery, but it might help. It was unlikely that Daisy would recover the use of her left arm and leg because the weakness and paralysis had persisted for so long. But I added what I told many other parents, "If this were my child, I would take the chance!" Her mother agreed and I quickly made arrangements, considering this a semi-emergency.

I performed an operation that I had never done before. I made two curved incisions over the temporal areas (beside the

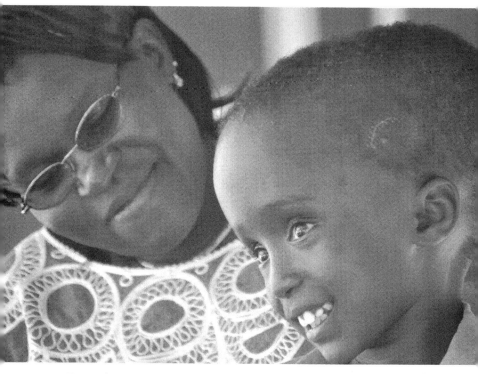

Emma (Daisy's mother) and Daisy

eyes) of Daisy's skull, drilled holes, and made incisions in the dura (membrane surrounding the brain). Out came fluid on both sides. I inserted drainage tubes on each side connecting them to sterile bags. I put a temporary suture around her shunt to stop the drainage and to allow the brain to fill the void in her skull. Her brain cortex was not thick prior to the recent insult and I hoped that this might expand the ventricles, pushing the brain out against the dura.

The operation complete, I sat down in the operating room to write my orders and a description of the operation. I regularly glanced over my shoulder at Daisy. I really had little hope of improvement and less hope for early evidence of improvement. But still I waited. And waited.

Suddenly she began to awaken. To my utter surprise she began moving her left arm and leg. Wow! I thought. Isn't God good?!

I hastily returned to the ward and shared the good news with Daisy's mom. What a joy that was! My heart was so thankful as I walked back up the hill toward home.

How We Got to Africa

CHAPTER 1

Stumbling Toward a Dream
(1944-1964)

"The heart of a man plans his way, but the LORD establishes his steps." Proverbs 16:9

I grew up in southern California. In 1944 my Mom, Dad, older brother Jack, and I lived in a small, two-bedroom duplex in a neighborhood full of other mirror-image duplexes. We didn't have a garage, just a cement slab to serve as a foundation if we could ever afford to build one. Our home was not far from Orange County. On spring nights the groves filled the air with the delightful fragrance of orange blossoms.

During my early years, World War II was raging.. There was some concern that the west coast of the U.S. was vulnerable to Japanese attack. Consequently, we experienced frequent air raid practices requiring "blackouts" where all the lights in every home in the community had to be extinguished. One night my Dad forgot to turn off our porch light during the blackout and an over-enthusiastic air raid warden broke the porch light to enforce the blackout. Another night, not far from our home, something big dropped from a passing plane. Thankfully, it wasn't a bomb. These incidents made many anxious.

The war also meant victory gardens[1], ration stamps[2], sacrifice, savings bonds[3], and hushed talk about relatives or friends who had died in battle. A stern "Uncle Sam"[4] pointed his finger from a poster at passers-by over the caption "Uncle Sam needs you!" Me, a kid?

When I was thirteen I began attending a Christian and Missionary Alliance (CMA) church. I confess I went primarily because two young ladies invited me. But the invitation truly came from the Lord. Even though I had attended Sunday school elsewhere for several years, most of what I learned hadn't really touched my heart. I knew very little about a personal God and nearly nothing about personal sin and the sacrificial love of God. But at this small church, I committed my life to Jesus Christ. Within the year I felt that the Lord's primary purposes for my life were to be an effective Christian, become a doctor, and work abroad among the poor as a missionary.

Medicine was advancing in the 1950s. Salk and Sabin made vital discoveries in developing polio vaccines. My home was not far from Rancho Los Amigos where the historic iron lung[5] was extensively used to save lives during the polio epidemics. March of Dimes polio posters featured children with leg braces and crutches. At school we were given small cards in which to collect dimes for research. I carried them home and proudly pushed the little coins into the slits. To me, eradi-

---

1 Small plots of land provided to citizens for cultivating vegetables for personal and community use.
2 Coupons for items that were in short supply.
3 Debt securities issued by the government to help fund its needs.
4 Initials "U.S.," a common national personification of the US government.
5 Medical ventilator enabling a person to breathe when muscle control is lost.

cating polio also meant that the community swimming pool, closed during the epidemics, could be reopened.

When I was 15 years old, I was given polio vaccine. A sign showing a bent hypodermic needle hung above the reception area in the doctor's office with the caption, "This one flinched." I didn't want to flinch; but I sure wasn't looking forward to that shot. When it came to needles, I was a coward. Funny characteristic for an aspiring doctor!

I was not an exceptional student. By fifth grade, I realized I could do reasonably well if I spent a lot of time studying, much more time than many of my peers. So with intense study habits, not innate intelligence, I graduated eleventh in a class of about 700 students at Compton High School. During the summer after high school, I took Algebra and Psychology at Compton College, a community college a few miles from my home. In the fall, I became a full time student taking as many undergraduate courses as possible before transferring to UCLA in September 1960.

While at Compton College, I joined Circle K, a collegiate service club associated with Kiwanis. The following year, I became president of that club. I also served as the president of both the Christian club we had begun the previous year and the Inter-Club Council. I knew these extra activities would look good on my medical school applications, but that's not what motivated me to participate. I genuinely enjoyed them.

My family was financially comfortable, but not by any means wealthy. I had sold Christmas and birthday cards from door-to-door for several years prior to college. From 1958 to 1960, I worked a variety of jobs to help make ends meet. I worked in a pharmacy, cleaning, stocking, and manning the checkout counter. I had a stint as a stock boy in a hardware store. At one point, I even sold men's clothing.

During my second year of college I worked as an orderly at St. Mary's Hospital in Long Beach, usually from 3 to 11 PM on Fridays and Saturdays. Although it had a detrimental effect on my social life, this was a wonderful experience, with the exception of two occasions. The first occurred when a sailor arrived at the hospital after a fight, bleeding profusely from what was later found to be a small cut on his face. As he was examined, I began to feel faint. A nurse noticed, tapped me on the shoulder, and suggested that I sit down. She was right. It was better to sit down than to fall down. The second occasion happened when a policeman came in with a gunshot wound. Again, I got dizzy and needed to sit down.

These two small incidents didn't discourage me from my dream of becoming a doctor. There were no medical people in my family who could inspire or mentor me toward this goal, but at St. Mary's I met Dr. Churchill, a young surgeon who had just entered practice. He was supplementing his income by working part time in the emergency room. He was kind and explained to me what he was doing and what he was thinking while caring for patients. At that time patients were charged $1.00 per stitch, and he often asked me to count the stitches so he would know what to charge. I'm sure that helped me get accustomed to watching wound repair.

I entered UCLA in the fall of 1960 to major in Physics. I lived in a co-op – a.k.a. the "COOP." At the co-op each person had a job. Initially I washed dishes. Later I helped cook and serve food a few days per week. I learned vital new skills such as how to squeeze a tea bag with a spoon, how to crack an egg with one hand, and how to make chocolate pudding. I became very good at making chocolate pudding.

In the second semester of my junior year I began attending Campus Crusade meetings. Often these were held in fraternity houses. Bill Counts, the Campus Crusade leader, asked me if I would consider coming to special classes on evangelism held on Thursday evenings. Usually Thursday was my day to cram because many of my exams occurred on Friday. I made several excuses, but I told him I would pray about it. Finally I agreed to attend. I committed to memorize Scripture, and learn how to present "The Four Spiritual Laws," an evangelistic tract created by Campus Crusade. It has been effectively used for several decades to help lead people into a personal relationship with Jesus Christ.

I also prayed about my very tough academic load. This was the term prior to applying for medical school. My grades that semester would be the most important grades on my application. God was faithful and kind. At the end of that term I received all A's and one B. I took the MCAT - Medical College Admission Test – an admission requirement at that time meant to be a "general knowledge" exam for pre-med students. I was not aware of anyone formally preparing for it. Most just took it and hoped to do well.

My senior year was a blur. I needed to take two or three upper division physics courses each semester to graduate. My girl friend had transferred from Compton College to UCLA. We would often study in the medical library until it closed and then retreat to the basement and continue studying until nearly midnight. I'm not sure why I decided to major in Physics. It was very difficult. But I thought Physics would open the door to many more professions than a pre-med degree, just in case I was not accepted into medical school.

The final exam in electromagnetics was two days before

graduation. The teacher was tough – really tough – and most of us felt we failed most of the tests. Many of us walked into the classroom for that final exam with much "fear and trembling." The professor began by announcing, "Anyone who believes he is going to graduate in two days should sign this paper!" I signed the paper. I got a C in the class. I believe that grade was a gift. I was thankful just to pass and be able to move on toward medical school.

I submitted thirteen applications to medical schools, including the University of California, Los Angeles (UCLA); University of Southern California (USC); University of Utah; University of Cincinnati; University of Tennessee; University of Chicago; University of Illinois; University of California, Berkeley; and Johns Hopkins. UCLA was the most comfortable choice for me. California was familiar to me. My home was there. My church was there. My friends were there. And my girlfriend, whom I had been dating for three years, was there.

But deep down inside, my dream was to attend Johns Hopkins in Baltimore, Maryland, considered to be one of the top medical schools in the U.S. I had read that it was the prototype for many of other medical schools in the country. I thought it was the best place in the world, but I was convinced that I would never get in. My girlfriend suggested I apply and, because the application fee was only $5.00, I did.

All of my interviews, including the ones for the University of Chicago and Hopkins, were in the Los Angeles area. For my UCLA interview I was directed to Dr. Stanley Wright's office where I tremulously knocked on the door. Recognizing my apprehension, he suggested that we go to the cafeteria for a cup of coffee. I was so nervous that I don't remember anything about that meeting. When we returned to his office, he suggested that I inform him if I was accepted to another medical school. This might allow him to speed up my acceptance to UCLA. He commented, "They are very slow!"

I received the University of Chicago's acceptance letter first and was absolutely thrilled. I dutifully returned to Dr. Wright's office to tell him. He commented that it was still too early to press for UCLA's acceptance. So I delayed my response to Chicago. My second acceptance came from Johns Hopkins. When I returned to his office, he shocked me by saying, "Go to Hopkins!" He said that UCLA would prepare me to be a good doctor, but Hopkins would provide me with the opportunity to experience a wonderful school in a new culture.

I was totally unprepared for that response. Even though my dream was to be able to go to Hopkins, my security, my family, and my girlfriend – my whole life – was in California. I really didn't like the idea of leaving this secure environment, but I was too proud to ask Dr. Wright to just let me go to UCLA.

So I made the noblest excuse that I could think of: "I can't afford it."

He responded, "I will write and get you a scholarship." With that, my last excuse was obliterated. I committed to attend Johns Hopkins.

Shortly before I departed for Baltimore, many of those in my church youth group gathered for my "going away" party. We had been spiritual brothers and sisters since my junior high days. They gave me a Scofield Reference Bible with my name engraved on it.[6]

6 It has been 53 years since I received that Bible. It has been to Africa and back. Tattered and worn, it sits on the bookshelf in my office.

On my day of departure, my parents, my girlfriend, and my best friend took me to Union Train Station in downtown Los Angeles. My best friend promised to look after my girlfriend in my absence. I boarded the train feeling very alone and a bit anxious. As I rode the rails, the Union Pacific changed to the Southern Pacific, which ultimately changed to the Baltimore and Ohio. I arrived in Baltimore, a big city hundreds of miles further east than I had ever been, my new home.

I disembarked, collected my suitcases, and hailed a cab. I had never been in a cab. The driver, possibly sensing my naïveté, drove me down Baltimore Street, arguably the city's worst street. I was wide-eyed and shocked at what I saw, from the strip joints to the rescue missions.

Finally we arrived at Reid Hall, located across the street from Johns Hopkins Hospital. I didn't know a soul in Baltimore when I arrived. I moved into my 8 x 10 foot room with a built-in bed, closet, and desk. Let's say it was "efficient." Within a few days I began classes with 74 classmates who seemed to be much, much smarter than I. But I was finally at Hopkins.

Johns Hopkins Hospital's main entry is a historic rotunda, housing a beautiful statue of Christ. Matthew 11:28 is written on this statue's base: "Come unto me all ye who are weary and heavy laden and I will give you rest." I passed that statue nearly every day on my way to class. What comfort those words proved to be.

Medical school began well. Biochemistry was hard. Anatomy included a lot of memorization, which was not one of my strengths. So, needless to say, I was working very hard to hold my own.

I wrote to my girl friend every day and received a letter from her every day. Initially, these were encouraging. But after

Statue of Christ in Rotunda of Johns Hopkins Hospital

a while her letters arrived less frequently. By October I received what is traditionally referred to as a "Dear John" letter. She told me she was engaged to my best friend. Or should I say my former best friend, the same friend who saw me off at Union Station in LA and promised to take care of her. He surely did!

I wish that I could say that I just shrugged this off. I didn't. I was crushed. My academic performance dipped significantly and I struggled the rest of the year.

One day a nursing student asked me if I would like to attend an "IV meeting" with her. Being a medical student, I thought possibly she meant "intravenous." Wrong! It was InterVarsity Christian Fellowship, a group for Christian students. I knew about Campus Crusade from my time at UCLA, but I had never heard of InterVarsity. So I attended with her and eventually became involved. Over the next year I became one of the small group Bible study leaders, which was great training for me.

I also began attending Central Presbyterian Church in Towson. The pastor, Murray Smoot, had once planned to go to China as a missionary. But when China abruptly closed its doors to missionaries, Murray changed directions and became a pastor. Over the years he became a good friend, mentor, and teacher.

As the Christmas vacation approached, I made plans to fly to Los Angeles. This was to be my first flight ever. On the morning of my trip, snow began to fall. Being a Southern California boy, I had seldom seen snow. I was thrilled to watch it cover the neighborhood. The impoverished and dirty area of Baltimore became white — all looked beautiful and refreshingly clean.

As soon as our last class concluded, a friend and I took a taxi to the Baltimore and Ohio Railroad station and caught the train to Washington National Airport in D.C. As we rode along the snowy tracks, I noticed a flare at each switch, apparently meant to keep them from freezing. The falling snow and the bright flames created a surreal scene - an enchanted wonderland to me.

However, as beautiful as it was, snow and flights don't mix well. Due to the bad weather, numerous flights were cancelled. Many of the passengers booked on those flights directed open anger toward the innocent flight clerks. It was bedlam.[7]

Miraculously, my flight was not cancelled. I boarded the plane trying to look like an experienced traveler. I fastened my seat belt and watched carefully as the flight attendant explained all of the emergency procedures. I took note of the emergency exits when she pointed to them, thinking that I might need to use one. The plane taxied to the runway and waited, but the wait took too long. The pilot had to go back to a hangar to have the wings de-iced. Finally, we taxied to the runway and took off.

I had no idea a flight could be so rough. As a novice, this was very unnerving. I looked for a "black bag," but fortunately didn't have to use one. My food stayed down, although I must admit I was afraid and uncomfortable.[8]

My return flight was also an adventure. We made twelve landings along the way. Yes, 12. It was a cheap flight. Eventually I arrived back in Washington, D.C., and embarked upon a new year, with a lot of unknown, and some unwelcome, events ahead of me.

The rest of the school year flew by. In the summer I returned to my home in California. I commuted back and forth from Compton to UCLA Medical Center where I did research on the dermatoglyphics[9] of patients with various genetic abnormalities. The study was under the oversight of Dr. Stanley Wright, the same pediatrician who had procured my scholarship to Hopkins.

---

7 In my last fifty-plus years I have never experienced anything similar to what I witnessed at the airport that evening, even though I have made hundreds of flights since that day.
8 My thoughts went to Wilbur and Orville Wright and their struggle to get their plane into the air for just a few seconds. I recalled the old adage "If people were meant to fly, God would have given them wings." To this day, I confess that I still don't totally understand how a plane can fly – and I majored in physics at UCLA!
9 The patterns of skin ridges on the lower surface of the hand or foot; the scientific study of fingerprints.

My job required frequent travel to Pomona to a special hospital for the disabled, many with congenital chromosomal abnormalities. I fingerprinted patients and returned to UCLA to decipher the prints and look for some consistent patterns that might help medical workers identify patients with genetic abnormalities. I enjoyed my work and was particularly content to do research with Dr. Wright.

One day our doorbell rang. I answered it and signed for a registered letter addressed to me. It was from Johns Hopkins. With butterflies in my stomach, and fearing the worst, I anxiously opened it.

I had failed.

The letter informed me that I had not performed well enough in my first year of medical school to advance to the second year of studies. However, the dean encouraged me to return to Hopkins, repeat my first year and hopefully continue on for my MD. In essence, I was invited to start over.

I was devastated. I had never failed at anything. I didn't know what to think of this interruption of God's "perfect plan" for my life. I questioned God. I irrationally asked Him how He could allow such a thing to occur. I complained to Him about this one-year delay of my work as a missionary doctor.

Many thoughts bounced around in my head. Why hadn't I chosen a school that was less academically challenging? I felt that I might have thrived at such a school. Or why hadn't I attended a school nearer home? In that case, I wouldn't have had the stresses of being far from home and family, the drastic lifestyle changes, and, of course, the damage to my friendships, including the end of my relationship with my girlfriend.

But I would not allow myself to indulge a "what if?" pity

party. I was an adult. I wanted to be a doctor. I had proudly made the choice to attend Hopkins. I wanted to serve God abroad. I wanted to be His man, even if I didn't like everything He was allowing in my life at the time. And, if I was brutally honest (though I did not like being that honest), the problem was me. I was the one who had failed.

It occurred to me that the easiest escape for my bruised ego would be to drop out of medical school entirely. I could avoid the embarrassment of seeing my former classmates who were all moving on to the next level without me. I shared this with my brother Jack. He welcomed me to join his contracting business if I didn't want to return to medical school. However, he also challenged me. He told me that if medicine was what I really felt called to do, I should return, face the music, and run after my dream.

Shortly thereafter I made my decision. I would return to Hopkins. I would face my former classmates. I would attempt to do whatever was necessary to graduate from the Johns Hopkins School of Medicine. I would swallow my pride and carry on.

At the end of the summer, I boarded a Greyhound bus and began my second journey to Baltimore. The train journey the previous summer had been slow, but the bus seemed to crawl along. Yet it gave me plenty of time to process the previous year's losses and try to optimistically anticipate what might lie ahead.

I had seen my first change of seasons in Baltimore. Not only had the seasons changed, but I too had changed.

This time, leaving California felt like I was truly leaving a major part of my life behind. This was hard in many ways. The term "cutting ties" comes to mind. Cutting is often traumatic. Life would never be the same. California was no longer my home; Baltimore was. I never returned to my childhood home in Compton after that summer. Most of my friends in California were now history. But many new friends were on my doorstep. I was learning new things at church and learning new things, both medically and spiritually, at Hopkins.

I would soon write this quote in my Scofield Bible:

"Man's disappointments are God's appointments."

Dr. Phillips, October 29, 1964 (possibly quoting from a poem)

During this year of re-entry, I continued to attend a weekly Bible study in Reid Hall. The group consisted of men and women from very different Christian backgrounds. None of us were experienced in leading Bible studies, but we took turns; we enjoyed our fellowship and worked hard to encourage one another.

Many of us participated in medical clinics at the Helping Up Mission and the Green Street Mission. We were overseen by "real" doctors from the community. We assisted in caring for patients by taking medical histories, taking vital signs, and doing physical exams. We would try to make a diagnosis and plan treatment before presenting the patient to the real doctor. Each week we saw between 15 and 50 patients at the rescue mission, mostly men who were down on their luck. Many were alcoholics. Some had once been successful but had experienced some tragedy in their lives. I learned a lot about myself, sharing my faith, and desperate people during that time.

In early 1964, InterVarsity Christian Fellowship had a missionary speaker at its annual spring retreat. The speaker challenged us to consider attending InterVarsity's Missionary Camp that summer. The speaker was persuasive, but, as

I tucked the brochure into my Bible, I pushed the camp idea into the back of my mind. Impossible! I had neither the time nor the money to attend.

Soon thereafter someone reminded me of a quote by Hudson Taylor, the founder of the China Inland Mission. Taylor said, "I have found that there are three stages in every great work of God. First, it is impossible. Then it is difficult. Then it is done."[10] Was there a lesson to be learned here?

I had already planned to be in Baltimore that summer, working on a project with one of the community health doctors. We would be reviewing the outcomes of pregnancies in young teenage mothers in the inner city. I would identify those who had delivered at Hopkins, visit them in their homes and gather data: age, parity, marital status, and details about the fathers of the children. The study would take eight to ten weeks to complete.

But the missionary camp idea kept coming back to me. To confirm that I would not be able to attend, I asked the health project leader if it might be possible for me to go to camp for four weeks and still have sufficient time to complete the study. Fully expecting him to deny my request, I was astonished when he told me that it would be possible.

So one obstruction was removed. However, I still had no money for such a frivolous adventure. But perhaps this was my opportunity to once more trust God. So I committed to go to the camp, not knowing how I would pay for it. Foolish? Perhaps. But the Lord seemed to be quietly inviting me to attend. It was a step of faith, part of a learning experience that would be repeated innumerable times in the future.

---

10 Lyall, Leslie T. 1976. *A Passion for the Impossible: the continuing story of the mission Hudson Taylor began.* London: OMF Books.

In June, a friend and I took a bus from Baltimore to Hagerstown to meet three other attendees. A nurse was driving up from Virginia with Millie Babb who had just finished her junior year as a math major at the College of William and Mary. The five of us were to meet at the bus station and share expenses on the drive together to the upper peninsula of Michigan. I usually describe this, tongue-in-cheek, as the time I was "picked up" in a bus station.

The five of us piled into the car and were off. We drove across Pennsylvania and Ohio, spent one night at a B&B in Michigan, and arrived in Cedarville late the following afternoon.

The first order of business was an interview of each attendee by camp leaders to determine if everything was in order. Millie and I waited together. Being the gentleman that I was, I suggested that she go first. When she came out, I went in.

What happened next is a perfect example of how God has amazed me with His provision and care. During college Millie had taught Sunday school at the Naval Weapons Station Chapel near Yorktown, Virginia. They generously provided the funds she needed for camp. But Inter-Varsity had also provided a scholarship for her. Since she didn't need the second scholarship, she declined it. As a result, the camp had extra funds that they did not have before her interview. They gave those funds to the attendee who came in after her. Me!

The "impossible" was done. My camp fees were fully paid. I was learning that God was sufficient.

The month was a flurry of learning about missions in Europe, Latin America, and Asia, boating and swimming, stargazing, evangelizing in surrounding towns, walking…and a little bit of romance.

Dr. Raymond Buker and his wife Dorothy, former missionaries to Burma, were speaking at the camp. They noticed that Millie and I were getting along very well. They subtly arranged for us to spend more time together, including reserving seats for us at their table for nearly every meal. On some evenings, Dr. Buker took attendees outside to look at the constellations. Millie seemed genuinely interested in the stars. Me? I was primarily interested in being under the stars with her.

Although we both wanted to do mission work, I hadn't decided on a particular region of the world. But Millie had. She felt God was directing her to Africa. I quickly recognized that I might be happy in Africa too – with the proper companion, of course. By the end of camp, we were more than casually interested in one another.

I invited Millie to come to Baltimore. She agreed to visit on her way back to Virginia. I began my return trip to Baltimore a few days before camp ended. I had a ride as far as Rochester, NY. I hitchhiked from there to Baltimore. A few days later, Millie arrived at the Baltimore bus station. Although it had only been a short time since we parted at camp, it seemed to me as if it had been a lot longer.

We walked and talked and learned much more about each other during that visit. Millie had been successful at teaching Sunday school and was preparing to be a teacher. At the same time, I seemingly had no particular interest in, or giftedness toward, working with kids. If someone had told me at that time that I would one day be thrilled to work with disabled kids, I would have thought them foolish. I wanted to be a general surgeon, or possibly an obstetrician. But God had other plans; He had just not mentioned them to me yet. He had a mission in mind and would ultimately give me the privilege of participating in His program.

I showed her around Johns Hopkins Hospital. She saw the statue of Christ in the rotunda. We attended the InterVarsity summer Bible study where I showed off my "new missionary candidate friend." As our time together came to an end, I eagerly agreed to come to Ivor, Virginia, to meet her family. That would be scary, but the anticipation of being with her again made the scariness worthwhile.

In August I took the bus to Ivor and met her parents. The Babb home was a bustling place. Some of their relatives often spent part of the summer at their home. Men boarded there while working on the power lines. They had a huge backyard garden with lots of dogs and cats. Their life was just busy, busy, busy. But in the midst of this busy-ness, they warmly welcomed me. Although I did not know it then, her family life and career choice would prove to be the perfect preparation for our future life together.

CHAPTER 2

Getting My Feet Wet (1964 – 1972)

"... I have learned in whatever situation I am to be content. I know how to be brought low, and I know how to abound. In any and every circumstance, I have learned the secret of facing plenty and hunger, abundance and need. I can do all things through him who strengthens me." Philippians 4:11-13

Many houses in Kijabe, Kenya, were built of stone that was mined nearby. One could see masons trimming pieces of stone with an ax. First they slowly chipped away the rough edges. Then they mortared them together to build a sturdy wall. Finally, they spread plaster on the inside surface, smoothing and covering all the defects.

Similarly, God, my divine Master Stonemason, was chipping away my worst rough edges and covering many of my flaws. My developing relationship with Millie was a big part of that process. Her quiet humility, her prayer life, and her hunger for God's Word were treasures hidden to most and deeply inspiring to me.

After she returned to the College of William and Mary to begin her senior year as a math major, we corresponded frequently. In September, I visited her in Williamsburg, a beautifully restored city that was once the capital of the American colonies. She was my own personal tour guide, and together we explored all the historic buildings up and down Duke of Gloucester Street. We ate at a colonial-style restaurant and attended a college football game. The weekend went by far too quickly.

At the end of September she returned to Baltimore for a second visit. Before that weekend was over, I proposed marriage. I didn't even have money to buy a ring. I had not completely thought about all the details, but was thrilled when she agreed to be my wife. I had no idea how we could afford to get married or where we would live. We were excited about pursuing God's plan for our lives together, wherever and however He might lead us. We believed that He would work out all of the details.

By late November, I was finally able to buy her a ring. I wrapped it in small box that I placed in the bottom of a much larger box. I included the letters she had written to me, plus a tiny baby basket with a baby boy and a baby girl in it. I marked the girl with the number 14 and the boy with the number three, because we had discussed having 14 daughters and three sons. It was entertaining to watch her carefully search through the big box for the tiny one containing her engagement ring.

I spent Christmas with Millie's family. Her father had passed away in November, so it was a bittersweet holiday. The day after Christmas we traveled to Richmond to join a large group of college students going to the InterVarsity Missionary Conference at the University of Illinois campus in Urbana, Illinois. This bus ride gave us extra time to talk and just be together.

Over 100 Christian mission organizations had set up booths in the school armory. Millie and I systematically visited every mission with a medical ministry in Africa. We enjoyed hearing biblical expositions by Dr. John Stott and presentations by other missionary statesmen. One morning during Dr.

Millie and Dick, 1964

Stott's lecture, a peculiar-looking man arrived just after us, wearing an overcoat, dark glasses, and a hat. He climbed the stairs to the top of the stadium, sat and listened. When the session was over, we discovered that it was Dr. Billy Graham attending incognito. He didn't want to detract attention from Dr. Stott and his teaching.

At the New Year's Eve service we, along with hundreds of other students, filled out pledge cards declaring our intention to commit ourselves to full-time missionary work. It was more than just a signature on a card. We were pledging our hearts, convinced that the Lord had put His hand on us to be His for the rest of our lives. We greeted 1965 with Communion and prayer and then boarded our bus for the return trip to Virginia.

In January, I began the introductory courses to clinical medicine. Hurrah! We wore our white coats quite proudly and were beginning to feel like we were almost doctors. Stethoscopes and small black books were tucked into our pockets. Millie and I continued to correspond and visit one another. I joked with her that I could not marry her until she could afford to support me. Although I said it jokingly, in reality, it was true.

Millie graduated from William and Mary in June 1965. Our wedding took place two weeks later, on June 26, 1965. Two days before the ceremony Millie and I, my parents, and my brother, Jack, and his wife played tourist in Williamsburg. When we were returning to the car, I lifted the camera to my eye to take a picture and promptly knocked out my contact lens. We eventually found it, but it was badly crushed. I couldn't replace it in time for the wedding. When Millie walked down the aisle, my vision was so blurry that I was uncertain if it was really Millie until she was halfway to the altar!

We experienced a bit of "financial déjà vu" as we considered our honeymoon. I had had no funds for missionary camp and nothing for a ring. Now we had no funds for a honeymoon. We didn't share this need with anyone. However, thanks to gifts from friends, we were actually able to enjoy a brief but happy honeymoon in Cape Hatteras on North Carolina's coast.

We returned to Baltimore and moved into our row house at 806 North Broadway, two blocks from Johns Hopkins Hospital. I did autopsies at Union Memorial Hospital that summer with a salary of $150 per month. I also worked as a phlebotomist to supplement our meager income. During that summer Millie decorated our apartment, and we began life together as husband and wife.

Though happily married, we were living hand-to-mouth that summer. Each month we drew down our checking account balance to less than a dollar. We ate whatever was cheap. Hot dogs were cheap, but chitterlings (pig intestines) were even cheaper.

Millie had been hired to teach mathematics at Towson Town Junior High. However, her job didn't begin until September and her first paycheck wouldn't arrive until the end of the month.

When my school year resumed in September, I had a medical rotation at Baltimore City Hospital. I was on call every third night and away from Millie on those nights. Our apartment was on Broadway, two blocks from Johns Hopkins Hospital, in an area of row houses that had once housed the middle and upper class of Baltimore. But by the 1960's, the neighborhood had deteriorated into an area of run-down tenement homes. Civil Rights marches were occurring in the South, and Americans were still finding it difficult to appreciate one another on the basis of character, not skin color.[11] Race relations were strained, especially in neighborhoods like ours, and being alone at night was stressful for Millie.

On one occasion, when she seemed particularly concerned, I thought long and hard about my responsibility as a husband and my love for my new wife. I knowingly told her that I was

---

11 In April, 1968, less than a year after we left Baltimore, riots occurred in the exact location where we had lived. These occurred within days after the assassination of Martin Luther King, Jr. Thousands of National Guard troops and 500 state policemen were called in to quell the violence. Eventually federal troops were requested. This was the same neighborhood in which I had left my wife of a few weeks in 1965.

prepared to quit medical school if she felt that this would be best. I wanted her to feel safe and she was far more important to me than medical school. Maybe that was all she needed to hear, because she quickly declared that she did not want me to quit.

Meanwhile, we continued to search for the right mission and the right location. A former roommate told me about Smith, Kline and French Fellowships that allowed medical students to spend summers in the developing world working in mission hospitals. I thought that I had little chance of receiving one of these fellowships because I had failed my first year of medical school. However, with Millie's encouragement, I applied for a fellowship in Africa.

The first requirement of the fellowship was to find a doctor working in the developing world to oversee my time there. I wrote to three doctors. To my complete surprise and joy, Dr. Bill Barnett agreed to allow me, an anxious, inexperienced, naive medical student about whom he knew nearly nothing, to assist him in Kijabe, Kenya.

Dr. Bill, as he is affectionately called, was born in Kenya and is practically a legend in East Africa. In 1907 his parents were among the early missionaries to go to Kenya. Bill, the youngest of six children, was born in 1917. When he began school he attended the relatively new Rift Valley Academy in Kijabe, which is now a well-known boarding school with approximately 500 students from many countries in Africa. To get there from their bush location, Bill rode in a Model T Ford to the railroad station, then boarded the East Africa Railroad that would take him to Kijabe. In previous years, transport to the train had been by ox cart and later the whole family rode on a motorcycle with a sidecar!

In his teen years he returned to the U.S. for further education. He completed his undergraduate work at Wheaton College. Dr. Billy Graham was one of his classmates and a close friend. Dr. Bill chuckles when he tells people that the closest he ever came to fame was cutting Dr. Graham's hair when they were students at Wheaton.

Dr. Bill is a man of many talents. During WWII, he attended Albany Medical College and enlisted in the U.S. Army. After internship and one year of surgical residency in Schenectady, NY, the army sent him to the hospital in Fort Bragg, North Carolina. During his year there, he was taught by a top-ranked orthopedic surgeon. Then he was shipped to the army hospital in Seoul, South Korea. On the day after his arrival he became the "chief of surgery." Because he was a doctor and an officer, he was later designated the Hospital Commander. Quite a promotion in a very short period of time! He humbly insists that this was due to the rapid turnover in the military at the time and not necessarily to his own talents. While there, Dr. Bill insisted upon, and initiated, care for sick Koreans employed by the army or injured by army personnel, a practice that had not been allowed before his arrival.

He returned to Africa in the early 1950s with his lovely wife Laura, who often assisted him in the operating room and was a source of constant encouragement. In 1966, he was the only full time doctor at Kijabe Hospital. Missionaries had founded this hospital in 1915 "to glorify God through compassionate health care provision, training and spiritual ministry in Jesus Christ."[12] I was thrilled to be invited to work with him. But there was a downside. We discovered that the fellowship would not pay for Millie to accompany me, since she was not

---

12 http://kijabehospital.org/

medical personnel. She urged me to go even if it meant that we would be separated for the summer.

Unbeknownst to us, Jim and Dottie Taylor were working behind the scenes at Central Presbyterian Church, informing others about this glitch in our plans. Jim was an engineer, and Dottie was a nurse. They were also volunteer sponsors for InterVarsity and the parents of four children. Millie and I knew them before we were married, and they were, in many ways, our mentors.[13] Through their efforts, people in the church provided the entire amount needed for Millie to accompany me. We were overwhelmed and grateful.

We departed from the Baltimore-Washington International Airport on June 25, 1966. This was Millie's very first flight. She was excited, and I was excited for her. We had a full day layover in London on June 26, our first anniversary! We had time to wander around the famous city that we had previously only read about in books. Excitedly we ate breakfast and then proceeded out to explore the city, and all its attractions. Early that morning we came upon a church with the name Westminster Chapel; the name sounded familiar to me. It was Sunday and the service had already begun. We entered the foyer and suddenly realized that Dr. Martyn Lloyd-Jones was the pastor. This was the man who wrote the book *Studies in the Sermon on the Mount*[14] that we used in our Inter-Varsity Bible study. He was, and is, one of my heroes, and now we could hear him in person. We were thrilled!

On our brief walk through London, we saw Buckingham Palace, Tower Bridge, St. Paul's Cathedral, Westminster

---

13 Years later Jim was the main person helping to found the International Rehabilitation Mission, Inc, a 501c3 initially created to help with my work with disabled children.
14 Lloyd-Jones, David Martyn. 1959. *Studies in the Sermon on the Mount*. Grand Rapids: Eerdmans.

Abbey, and the Tower of London. That evening we boarded our flight to Kenya. Shortly before arriving in Nairobi another passenger commented that a previous plane had mistakenly landed in the game park. That was a bit shocking. But our pilot didn't have any problem finding the runway and we landed safely at Jomo Kenyatta International Airport. Laura Barnett and two others met us as we disembarked.

We were in Africa, the continent of our dreams!

Dr. Bill Barnett was "on safari," which meant he was traveling to remote clinics to help nurses caring for patients sometimes with complex needs. In his absence, Dr. Bill had entrusted much of the work at the hospital into my inexperienced hands. I was the first medical student to come to Kijabe Hospital. Thank God the nurses knew far more than I did!

A few days later I entered the maternity ward to examine a woman in labor. I thought she had a ruptured uterus and that the baby was most likely dead. Because I had not yet had any hands-on surgical training, I quickly called the only other doctor at Kijabe, Dr. Ellen Norton. She came to the hospital and agreed with my diagnosis. Surgery was necessary, but the woman would likely need a blood transfusion. No compatible blood was available at the hospital at that time.

It was Sunday morning and the church service had already begun. Since we had only arrived a few days earlier, I had not yet attended that church. I entered the building, marched straight to the front, and announced that we needed blood donors. Several people volunteered. We returned to the hospital where I assisted Ellen in the operating room. Although she had never done this operation before, she was the only one available who had any chance of saving this poor lady's life.

Ellen delivered the dead baby and placenta and repaired the uterus. The patient recovered and soon went home.

Millie and I stayed busy the entire summer. She taught physical education, physics, and math at various institutions: RVA, Kijabe High School, and the Teacher Training College. I worked in the Kijabe Hospital for two months, at a remote hospital at Kapsowar for one month, and in the Northern Frontier for two weeks. Millie traveled with me most of the time.

While in the Northern Frontier of Kenya, my days were divided in half. In the mornings I helped build a road to a new mission station on Mt. Kulal. In the afternoons, I tried my hand at running a clinic, caring for a group of people called the Rendille. At that time, there were fewer than ten Christians among this people group. Evening devotions for the missionaries, volunteers, and other national workers required translations from English into Swahili, Samburu, and Rendille.

I also unexpectedly covered for a doctor at Lokori, a very remote Turkana village in northern Kenya. Little did they realize what a limited amount of medical training I had. But, alas, I was considered the only option for care for the people in the region while their real doctor was away on a medical safari.

The trip to Lokori was my first experience flying into the bush in a small plane with Mission Aviation Fellowship[15] (MAF). I arrived early at the MAF hangar at Wilson Airport in Nairobi and met a pleasant British pilot. I was the only passenger on his single-engine Cessna 206 when we departed from Nairobi.

15 https://www.maf.org/

Flying a single-engine plane is a bit of a risk. If that one engine fails, you are in a tough situation. After the signal "clear prop!" the engine sputtered – and I do mean sputtered - to life. We taxied down the runway, turned, and took off.

The pilot was very silent, intently listening to the engine. Then he abruptly made a wide circle and returned to Wilson Airport, saying, "The engine does not sound quite right!" Oh! I thought. He removed the cowling and listened to the engine again. He checked the oil and adjusted a few other things before explaining that the oil had recently been changed and that he thought that was causing the new sound. Reassured, or at least somewhat reassured, we got back into the plane. We took off and headed toward Nakuru, where we landed and added a few passengers.

But this time as we prepared to take off the engine wouldn't start at all. The pilot claimed it was due to a vapor lock and set about fixing it. Finally we were again in the air and headed toward Kapeddo. There we deposited the passengers and took off toward Lokori, my final destination.

What a week it was! I saw my first cases of leishmaniasis, a skin disease that most commonly causes skin sores, but which can be much worse.[16] One small girl with this condition need-ed a transfusion before she could be treated with a rather toxic medication. I soon realized that in such a remote place this would prove challenging. We used little cards of chemically reactive paper to determine that she was A-positive. Because I was A-negative, I seemed to be the best potential donor – or perhaps the easiest to convince. We had no way to cross-

---

16 *Leishmaniasis* is caused by infection of Leishmania parasites, which are spread by the bite of phlebotomine sand flies. The most common form is cutaneous leishmaniasis, which causes skin sores. The other main form is visceral leishmaniasis, which affects several internal organs (usually spleen, liver, and bone marrow) and can be life threatening.

match for any other blood factors. She would get A and that was the best we could do. Anticoagulant needed to be added, so we weighed out an approximate amount into a bottle and then sterilized it all in a pressure cooker similar to what my mom had used for beans. The method was primitive, but effective. We similarly sterilized a segment of red rubber tubing.

Then I experienced another first. I had to take my own blood. For someone with needle issues, this was a challenge. But I pushed the needle into my own vein – oh! – and watched my blood spill into the bottle. It was successfully transfused into the little girl.

The rest of the week was a blur. Before I knew it, it was time to leave. The airplane dutifully returned with the regular doctor and I was ready to add more flight time to my resumé. But again the airplane would not start. This time it was a dead battery. The plane needed to be jump-started. Funny sounds. Vapor lock. Dead battery. Was this the way airplanes were supposed to function, or was this just a bad week for aviation in Africa?

Eventually I returned safely to my young wife in Kijabe and resumed work with Dr. Bill. He helped me do my first Caesarian section and counseled me to pursue general surgery while adding extra coursework and clinical experience in obstetrics and gynecology. Much of who I am as a doctor is because of my friend Bill. My interest in the disabled, my dabbling in orthopedics and plastic surgery, my love for training young doctors and medical students – all were initially inspired by Dr. Bill Barnett.

After this whirlwind summer, Millie and I returned to Baltimore. She returned to teaching and I returned to studying and clinical work. It was my last year of medical school. In

June 1967, I graduated from Johns Hopkins with my MD, truly thankful that, years previously, I made that hard decision to return to medical school and stay the course to become a doctor.

We moved to Morgantown, West Virginia, where I did my internship and the first year of my surgical residency at the West Virginia University Medical Center. Our son, Chris, was born in 1968. He added a lot of joy to our family. We were new parents on a rapid learning curve. I continued to be on call in the hospital every second or third night. Millie was now a "stay-at-home" mom, often functioning as both Mom and Dad. I would snatch brief times between call and sleep to hold and rock our new baby boy.

Eventually I realized that continuing my surgical residency in Morgantown was not the best choice for me. Although the surgical training and teaching conferences were very good and most of the professors were considerate of the patients and trainees, I felt that the head of the surgical department was often inconsiderate of trainees. So in 1969 we moved to Omaha, Nebraska, to complete my surgical training. Although the academic program was perhaps not as challenging as the one that I had come from, the character of the staff in Omaha was more agreeable.

On a very cold January morning in 1970, our second son, Rick, was born. I was becoming increasingly busy in my medical work. I often would not see our boys awake from Monday through Friday. I usually left in the morning before they awoke and returned after they were in bed. But I did try to spend as much time as possible with them on the weekends.

In 1971, while still a surgical resident, I attended a leprosy conference in Carville, Louisiana where Dr. Paul Brand[17], a world-renowned leprosy surgeon, was the key speaker. A committed Christian, Dr. Brand was a joy to get to know. I would deeply appreciate his teaching years later when I encountered this devastating disease in Africa.

In 1972, during the final months of my general surgical residency, a letter arrived from Dr. Bill asking if I could come back to Kijabe to help with the surgical work for a few months. However, I was scheduled to enter the US Air Force that summer. I had registered for the draft when I turned 18. I had been given a 14-year deferment through college, medical school, and surgical residency. But that was now ending. (The Vietnam Conflict was winding down and crews from the B52s and KC135s would soon be returning.) I was to enter the U.S. Air Force as a surgeon at Fairchild Air Force Base, a Strategic Air Command base.

Although I thought it was probably a lost cause, I wrote the US Air Force explaining the situation and requesting another delay of my induction in order to help in Africa for part of the year. The answer surprised me. I was permitted to postpone entering the Air Force until the November induction, the last induction class for the year.

I approached Dr. Merle Musselman,[18] the head of the surgical department at the University of Nebraska Medical Center, and asked if I could accelerate my training, relinquish my vacation time, and complete my residency by the first part of

17 Wilson, Dorothy Clarke. 1989. *Ten Fingers for God: the Life and Work of Paul Brand.* Grand Rapids, Mich: Zondervan Publishing House.
18 Dr. Merle Musselman became one of my heroes. He was in the Philippines during World War II, was captured and part of the Bataan Death March. He spent three years as a POW and was liberated shortly after the Allied forces returned to the Philippines. I didn't learn the full details of this until 20-30 years after I left Nebraska. For more details, read "The Great Raid" in: Sides, Hampton, and James Naughton. 2001. Ghost soldiers [the forgotten epic story of World War II's most dramatic mission]. New York: Random House.

June. He was delighted to allow me to do this.

By April 1972 our home was for sale, and we began planning to leave for Africa in early June. We were not able to fully finance our trip but our church, the Omaha Gospel Tabernacle, realized this and accepted donations on our behalf.

The church was given enough to buy one-way tickets to Africa for our family of four, including three-year-old Chris and two-year-old Rick. The church also gave us a small amount to cover extra expenses. We hoped that the proceeds from selling our house would help us financially, but it didn't sell until after we departed. The total profit was only a few hundred dollars.

Those five months in Africa included two months in Kijabe, one month in Kapsowar, and then two months in Zaire (now the Democratic Republic of Congo, DRC). Many memories of those months flood into my mind. I remember opening the skull of a child to release the pressure of a blood clot following a fall from a tree. It was the first subdural hematoma I ever drained, and he recovered well. I wired a fractured mandible with fence wire, the only wire available. I saw numerous patients who had trephinations, the act of perforating the skull with a surgical instrument,[19] done by traditional healers. One of my patients went into cardiac arrest during a hysterectomy. She ultimately recovered. I also did a C-section on a mother whose infant had hydrocephalus.[20]

In September, one of the missionary doctors in Zaire brought his sons to RVA to resume school, and we accompanied him on his return trip to Nyankunde. We spent the night in Entebbe, Uganda, on our way to Zaire. That evening the local

---

19 Historically this was sometimes done in the belief that this would allow the healing of seizures and other mental diseases.

20 *Hydrocephalus* is a condition that occurs when fluid builds up in the skull and causes the brain to swell. Brain damage can result if it remains untreated.

news declared, "Western powers are trying to assassinate Idi Amin!" This tyrant was the President of Uganda at the time. Our hosts felt it would be best for us to leave Entebbe as soon as possible. So we departed early the next morning. On our way to the Zaire border, our host drove right through a police stop, the only time in all of my years in Africa that I ever saw someone completely ignore an armed roadblock.

When we arrived at the DRC border crossing, we waited over an hour until the border officials returned. Then we had the interesting experience of changing from driving on the left side of the road to driving on the right side. We traveled to Rethy, where a missionary academy and hospital were located, and then on to Nyankunde where the Centre Medical Evangelique, a cooperative effort of five mission societies, was located. This was the main hospital for all of Northeastern Zaire. Because I didn't speak French, the hospital staff decided to park me in the operating room where sleeping patients wouldn't require too much conversation.

Not long after we arrived, Millie contracted malaria and bacillary dysentery at the same time. Dr. Carl Becker[21], a well-known missionary doctor, kindly cared for her. He administered a morphine injection to treat the dysentery and gave her appropriate malaria medication. I personally didn't understand why she acted so sick and couldn't, or wouldn't, accompany the boys and me to dinner engagements. About a week later, I experienced my own first bout of malaria and immediately became much more sympathetic and understanding!

Huge flying cockroaches, the generator shutting down during a late-night C-section, wind blowing the roof off of

---

21 Petersen, William J. 1967. *Another Hand on Mine; the Story of Dr. Carl K. Becker of the Africa Inland Mission*. New York: McGraw-Hill. Dr. Becker oversaw the largest leprosarium in the world located at Oicha, DRC and had done some ingenuous research on leprosy.

the house in which we were living, and a child whose mother poured gasoline over his hands and set them on fire because he stole are all startling events that have left deep impressions of our time in Zaire.

Near the end of our time there, the border between Zaire and Uganda was closed. Radio communication was forbidden. We did find out that we had sufficient funds to pay for our return airline tickets, but we had no legal way to exchange money and buy those tickets in Zaire. Our only means of communication between Nyankunde and Uganda was by short-wave radio transmissions. Replies from Uganda had to be manually delivered across the border by a Ugandan man who traveled by bus to the crossing. Using this cumbersome method, friends in Kampala, Uganda purchased our return tickets.

At the last minute, the border re-opened, allowing a small MAF plane to carry our thankful family to Entebbe. This was the same plane that had taken us to Oicha where I had done surgical procedures and tried to advise a nurse about the care of leprosy patients. This plane also took us to a pygmy village where we felt like giants. And this was the plane taking us to the modern airport, allowing us to return to the familiar, safe, medically elite U.S., a land of plenty. We felt a rush of adrenaline as our plane climbed higher and we could look over the countryside. But we also felt nostalgic for all that was being left behind.

It had been a hard time in many ways, but an important eye-opening experience for me. My heart felt deep pangs of guilt when I thought of those without access to medical care, those who had never heard the Gospel, the poor, the needy, the destitute, and the hungry. Refugees and internally displaced people. Unaccompanied and orphaned minors. In time my thoughts would also include people trapped in war-torn countries like Somalia, Rwanda, and Sudan.

In Omaha, we packed our remaining possessions and sent them off to our next location: Fairchild Air Force Base near Spokane, Washington. Millie and the boys stayed with neighbors in Omaha while I went to San Antonio, Texas, where the Air Force tried to teach me and a group of doctors and dentists how to wear military uniforms, march, polish shoes, and salute.

After basic training, I returned to my family in Omaha, said goodbye to a wonderful three years of our lives, and began driving west. In western Nebraska it began to snow and Millie began to vomit. But this time it was not malaria. It was newly-conceived Bethany, who made my happy and helpful wife not only nauseous but absolutely exhausted. The snow turned into a blizzard as we cautiously made our way into Cheyenne, Wyoming, where we spent the night.

The following morning, with no snow falling, we continued our journey to Fairchild. When we arrived our house wasn't ready, so we stayed in a rather iffy motel where we stuffed a towel beneath the door to keep out the cold and left the oven door open to warm the frigid room.

But by Christmas we were in our home and a new chapter of our lives was about to begin.

I was getting more pediatric training too. With two small boys, I had mastered diapers and pins. I knew a little about childhood illnesses. But I was still not enamored with caring for sick children. They couldn't communicate, wore leaky diapers, and frequently exuded the sour odor of vomit. God still had quite a bit of work to do in me!

CHAPTER 3

Finding a Niche (1972 – 1982)

*"Come to me, all who labor and are heavy laden, and I will give
you rest. Take my yoke upon you, and learn from me, for I am
gentle and lowly in heart, and you will find rest for your souls.
For my yoke is easy, and my burden is light."*

Matthew 11:28-30

At 13, I had committed myself to following Jesus. At 14, I
felt God's leading to a career in missions. There was the feeling that everything was far in the future. With college and
medical school, marriage, and residency completed, the stage
was set for realizing long dreamed of goals. The "pieces" were
coming together.

Millie and I were still searching, still seeking, for what God
might have for our future. We pondered whether we should
return to Africa or consider working in Southeast Asia. Being
in the Air Force I could fly "stand by" on military planes. So
I took leave time to make an exploratory trip by U.S. Air
Force jet to Thailand to determine whether we should join the
Christian and Missionary Alliance work there.

Arriving at the leprosarium and Bible school at Khon Kaen
on a Sunday evening, I was taken to a memorable church service. A man whose feet were severely damaged due to leprosy
wanted to give his testimony. An almost fingerless fellow leper
lifted his friend and carried him to the front to speak. He said,

"I thank God for leprosy, for it is through this that I found the Lord!" I was truly humbled.

The next morning I spoke at the chapel service. I don't remember anything I said, but I do remember being asked what song I would like sung. I suggested "Take My Life and Let it Be."[22] I have never forgotten the second stanza of that song:

> *Take my hands and let them move*
> *At the impulse of Thy love.*
> *Take my feet and let them be*
> *Swift and beautiful for Thee.*

Imagine singing this beautiful hymn in a leprosarium!

Although it was a memorable trip I did not feel the Lord leading us to Asia. I really do not know why. Perhaps it is because mastering the language of the people group one hopes to serve is an important part of overseas outreach. Thai is a tonal language and I am nearly tone deaf. It would have been very difficult for me to master Thai and interact with the people.

Our daughter, Bethany Elise, was born on July 18, 1973. As our family expanded so did our vision for ministry. We felt God's leading to join Africa Inland Mission[23] (AIM). We attended Orientation School in Pearl River, NY, in July 1974, and learned that two surgeons were already preparing to go to Kijabe. The leadership of AIM asked if we would consider going to some Islands in the Indian Ocean, located off the coast of East Africa.[24] Europeans had colonized the country, yet, nearly all of its population was, and is, Muslim. It was a ripe, medically needy, unopened field and that appealed to us.

---

22 See Appendix for full lyrics.
23 http://aimint.org/
24 Unidentified for security purposes.

So we agreed.

In January 1975, two months after finishing my Air Force obligation, we were finally "on our way." On our way to where? To Neuchatel, Switzerland to study French for eight months. French was the trade language and language of education for both the Islands and Zaire.[25] I have often joked with friends saying, "If you have to suffer, suffer in Switzerland!" It is the land of chocolate, cheese, and magnificent mountains.

And study we did! We took the kids to pre-school and nursery school, studied French, fed the ducks at the port, studied French, opened our apartment to others who were studying French, spent our vacation times traveling around Switzerland on student tickets, and studied French. We moved from class to class maximizing our meager language skills before moving to Belgium where I studied tropical medicine - in French.

At this point AIM had changed our assignment and was strongly directing us toward DRC in spite of our expressed longing to go immediately to the Islands. Before any missionaries could depart for their work, they needed to be assigned to a country already "opened" to AIM work. When we departed from the U.S. for Switzerland, the Islands were not yet a "field" in AIM's eyes. The mission had therefore assigned us to DRC in order to fulfill one of their requirements regarding new missionaries. But while we were in Belgium, the Islands had become an official AIM field, but our assignment had already officially, in the eyes of the mission and the Zaire church, been finalized. I argued against this assignment, but Millie regularly countered my arguments with the admonition, "We are under authority!"

25 Now the Democratic Republic of Congo. The name was changed in 1997.

So on February 29, 1976 (a leap year), in spite of all my misgivings, we obediently departed from Brussels and flew to Kinshasa, Zaire. We arrived about 11 PM, expecting to meet a pre-arranged travel agent. He never appeared. We passed through immigration easily, but we couldn't exchange money at that time of night. We had no idea how to get from the airport to our accommodations at the Mennonite Guest House.

By now it was about 2 AM. A Congolese man advised us that we would need two taxis and that he could arrange this. We could pay him the following day. Foolishly, I asked Millie to travel in the second taxi with all three kids, while I traveled in the first taxi with the luggage and all of our passports. I sped away in the first taxi. Little did I know Millie's taxi had battery problems and needed to be push-started. Then they puttered along without headlights to conserve battery power.

My speedy taxi was stopped at a roadblock where drunken soldiers demanded to examine my papers. I showed them all of the passports and told them that my family was following me. But their taxi wasn't anywhere in sight.

That trip to Kinshasa was excruciatingly long. My family was somewhere back there in the unknown. I felt guilty about my poor decision. Of course, there's a happy ending to this story. Eventually we were back together again and safe. But it was a reminder to me to be more discerning in the future.

We spent a month in Kimpese and Kinshasa, during which we arranged for residency papers, applied for a medical license, and did a mini-internship. Then we flew 1200 miles over a huge tropical forest on our way to Nyankunde in northeastern Zaire.

Missionary Aviation Fellowship (MAF) later flew our family to Banda, where we were tentatively to be stationed. It was a remote station, really remote, among the Azande tribe. I was to be the only doctor. The mud roof in the second operating room had collapsed the day before we arrived. Equipment sterilization had been only recently moved from an outside pressure cooker over an open fire to a somewhat more modern inside unit. Fortunately we had running water, thanks to two 55-gallon barrels and pipes transporting the water directly into the operating room. The operating room lights were battery-powered. Honestly, Banda was everything I had not dreamed of.

A few weeks later, Millie and I met with the leadership of the Congolese church and were asked to share our testimony. At this time they would determine where we would actually be assigned. DRC is a very large country with very few doctors. Banda was hundreds of miles away from the nearest real hospital. They had needed, wanted, and prayed for a doctor for years. However, they told us that they had recently received a letter from Pastor Etsea, the head of CECA (roughly translated as The Evangelical Church of Congo), suggesting that the church leadership consider sending us to the Islands. He had attended a prayer meeting in Kenya while on his way to the U.S. and heard that the Islands were opening up and desperately needed help.

They learned that in the previous year, 30 of 36 doctors left the Islands when they declared unilateral independence from their colonial masters. So there was a limited medical presence and no evangelical witness at all. The leaders asked us how we felt about this. I confessed that I longed to serve in the Islands and Millie did too. Later that afternoon they called us back and told us that the Congolese church wanted us to go to the Islands as their missionaries. Although they felt that DRC had the greatest medical need, they concluded that the Islands had the greatest spiritual need. We thanked them and praised God. What an interesting, and humbling, turn of events! While I had strongly felt that we should have gone directly to the Islands in the first place, proceeding there with the blessing of the "authorities" over us was wonderful. That turn of events helped me to understand a bit more of God's plan and His ways.

We flew first to Nairobi and then on to the main island, which had a population of about 250,000. I often tell people, tongue-in-cheek, that I became the chief of surgery and the chief of obstetrics and gynecology at the main government hospital in the capital city. Although that was true and sounded impressive, in reality I was one of only two doctors in the 350-bed hospital in a desperately poor country. And I was the only surgeon on the island.

Medically, life was very busy. My skills were taxed immensely. I arrived at the hospital by 7 AM every day and was responsible for 150 beds. I scheduled operations to be done four days a week and saw outpatients one day a week. I made rounds on half of all surgical patients each day and saw all serious patients every day.

I was frequently called back in the afternoon or during the night for emergencies, especially at the end of mango season when pickers climbed further and further out on narrow, weak branches to get the last of the fruit. Consequently, the number of falls and fractures increased. Although I was not trained as an orthopedist, during that season I would often reduce three to five fractures each day and apply casts. I often pinned femoral fractures. Many, many times I felt out of my depth. To improve my skills I spent hours poring over medical books previously donated by a kind medical book salesman.

Children occasionally arrived with deformities due to polio, clubfeet, cleft lips, and other disabilities. While I casted some of the clubfeet, I had nearly nothing to offer the others with disabilities. I tried to send some to Kenya or Tanzania for bracing or operations, but most could not go. This was frustrating, to say the least.

In early April 1977, a volcano located in the center of our island began to spew ash and lava. We were 12 or 13 miles from the volcano, but from our kitchen window we could see molten lava erupting from the summit. The eruption continued for two weeks. The flow of lava divided our island in half. Steam rose from the ocean when the hot lava hit the water.

As if this was not enough, on April 12 the central government was dissolved. Many governmental services were discontinued. We had to pick up our mail at the prison. All municipal records were piled outside government buildings and burned. Even architectural plans, prison records, birth records, and employment records were destroyed. We were told that this was being done so the government could "begin over again."

Shortly thereafter a radio announcement abruptly informed us that the government was reducing the staff at our hospital. Then the announcer read the names of 106 of the 171 staff. Those 106 should no longer report for work. Suddenly, our 350-bed hospital was to be staffed by only 65 workers. Needless to say there were many irate people. I had had nothing to do with this announcement and was as surprised as everyone else. I met with the leadership of the surgical and obstetrics department, and we decided to perform only emergency operations until the situation was clarified. Some of the staff that had been relieved of their positions tried unsuccessfully to stop all work at the hospital.

Around this time I was informed that there would be a team of Italian doctors coming in June to replace me. While I was rather flattered that a "team" would replace me, I was also a bit disappointed. Millie and I had developed relationships and had established a routine. However, we were instructed to move to another island where I would be in charge of the main government hospital, replacing a local surgeon who was popular on that island, but not popular with the government. Another change and another challenge!

In June we flew back to Kenya because we were expecting

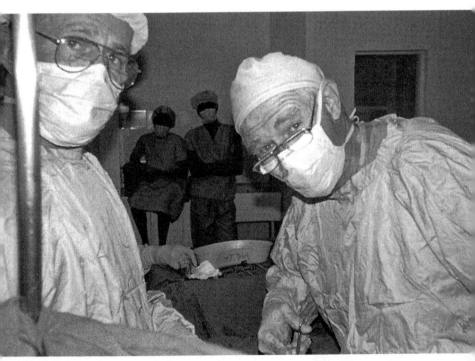

Dr. Bill Barnett and Dick in operating room on the islands, circa 1976

another addition to our family. Millie had O-negative blood, which was rarely found on the island. Since I was the only surgeon, I did not want to be responsible if a C-section were needed. Our children were excited about the new baby. Chris and Rick had prayed for a baby brother, and Bethany had prayed for a sister, and – surprise! - God gave us both! The twins, Jonathan and Susan, were born by C-section on July 11, 1977. We had no idea that we were having twins until they arrived. Millie and I agreed that Jon's middle name would be Luke. However, after I spent a full night of operating prior to going to have their births registered, I forgot and gave him the middle name Mark. That's the kind of thing that happens when I am sleep-deprived!

Upon our return, we relocated to the other island. We moved into a filthy house. Pigeons had nested in boxes suspended on the wall inside the kitchen. The birds exited through ventilation holes in the wall that opened onto the porch, so the porch was covered with pigeon droppings. Chickens pecked all around the property; roosters sat in the trees near our bedroom at night and crowed at the full moon, often commencing their announcement of dawn at 2 or 3 AM. And there were guinea fowl galore. The previous inhabitants owned six dogs, leaving behind an army of ticks that sometimes found their way to the mosquito netting over the baskets where the twins slept.

Millie was exhausted. Between the serenade of the roosters and trying to nurse twins, she had little time for sleep. Millie and Boina, the young man who helped in our home, used a wringer washer to do the laundry, a time-consuming chore made even more difficult because of the volume of soiled clothing generated by our infant twins. One day the clothesline broke and all the newly washed diapers fell in the dirt. And I mean dirt! Millie was literally "at the end of her rope" and ran to the hospital to inform me that she simply could no longer live on the Islands. But of course, I was in the O.R. and unavailable.

It was one of those turning-point moments for Millie. She returned home, calmed down and opened her Bible. God assured her that He had taken her to the new island for her own sake and that the "yoke she was to wear"[26] was custom-made for her by the master carpenter Jesus. She prayed, then resolutely rewashed the diapers, and recommitted herself to our assignment.

But we were not destined to remain there long-term after all. In October I became very sick and was treated for malaria three times with no resolution of symptoms. I lost 35 pounds. Our leaders decided that our family should be flown to Kenya where I would receive more advanced care. At Kijabe I was given tetracycline for possible tick typhus. I believe my temperature began to drop and my symptoms improved even as I took my first tetracycline capsule. I have often felt that God used this illness as a means to redirect us.

I returned briefly to the Islands alone in November. Due to island politics, the family stayed in Kijabe. Soon thereafter an event occurred that forced our whole team to leave the Islands. A couple from Haiti had joined our team. They had shared tracts and witnessed about their faith in ways that had drawn too much attention from the Muslim government. Consequently, they were jailed and then deported from the Islands. In January 1978 the authorities told all expats that they were not welcome if they wanted to share their faith. AIM decided that our organization should "go away" for a while. So in January 1978, I found myself packing what I could and flying back to Kenya.

---

26 Matthew 11:28-30

I was invited to join the long-term staff at Kijabe Hospital. At that time the hospital could accommodate 80-90 patients, although with significant crowding. There were four doctors in the hospital - two general surgeons and two generalists. Although I had worked at Kijabe[27] in 1966 as a medical student and had returned to help for two months in 1972, I still had a lot to learn.

One observation staggered me. The average local woman had eight children. It was my guess that an average of four of those children died before reaching adulthood, many in the first year of life. Why? Many died of diarrhea and respiratory infections, but an inordinate number succumbed to measles and whooping cough. I found myself desperately trying to prolong the lives of many of these little ones while seeking advice from anybody and everybody. Fortunately the hospital's maternal and child health program was just beginning and part of this program included immunizations. I believe immunization saved the lives of many children and helped prevent many other infectious diseases, including polio. Ultimately I was put in charge of this program.

Thirty to thirty-five of the beds at Kijabe were obstetric beds. The hospital wanted to initiate a nurses' training program, but needed 100 non-obstetric beds to qualify to do so. A building program to add those beds had begun the year before, so with the construction in progress, we were allowed to start the program.[28]

In our early days at Kijabe there was not much medical

---

27 Kijabe was, and is, a great place to live and work. It's located about halfway up the escarpment of the Great Rift Valley. The name Kijabe means "place of the wind" and on most evenings strong gusts surge down the forested slope as if in a hurry to reach the valley. The hospital is one of the earlier medical facilities on the continent. A small local village is perched on the hillside above the hospital and higher up is the K-12 school, Rift Valley Academy (RVA).

28 It would not be until about 1982 when the hospital would have the additional beds to meet the requirements for a full nurses' training program.

competition. By this I mean that there were so few surgeons in Kenya that if you were not practicing in the capital you could do almost any kind of surgical procedure, if you were bold, or foolish, enough to do so. Doctors who had had either little or no formal surgical training were doing surgical procedures throughout the country. There was a large, unmet need for surgical care. Thus, I soon became a kind of gynecologist-obstetrician, orthopedist, neurosurgeon, urologist, plastic surgeon, ENT, and you-name-it type of surgeon. We all did what we could do, recognizing that there were few affordable, accessible, better-trained surgeons in the entire country. I often looked at patients and wept inside. Many of them could have been cured in the West.

I did a lot - and I mean a lot - of reading about orthopedic procedures. I was very conservative in my days as the orthopedist. With the exception of fractured femurs, I did a limited number of elective open procedures. We had very few visiting orthopedists and no e-mail. Occasionally I took a textbook with good illustrations into the operating room and had it available at the bedside. I was literally doing surgery "by the book."

Eventually all of our kids walked 100 yards up the hill to Rift Valley Academy to attend school. They left home in the morning, came home for lunch, and went back in the afternoon. Millie taught Math and French there. All of our children were involved in school events and especially enjoyed participating in sports. Often their games or events were simultaneously held in different areas of the campus, which led to some creative juggling and shifting for Millie and me. But we agreed that it was important for both of us to cheer them on and support their efforts as much as possible.

I tried to plan my medical schedule weeks, sometimes months, ahead in order to attend these sporting events, choir concerts, and other assorted occasions. The days I operated were particularly challenging. Eventually I developed a workable method. I would walk into the O.R. in the morning and announce to the team (anesthetist, scrub techs, nurses), "I have an emergency at 3:30!" They would all smile because this was my code for "one of my kids is playing ball at 3:30." Thank God for an understanding staff! We all worked hard throughout the day, doing whatever we could to finish up all of the scheduled cases. I often picked up the mop and mopped the floor between operations to help move things along more smoothly. Usually, as the last case was being wheeled into the room, we would exchange smiles. We were nearing the point when we could say, "Mission accomplished!" With this teamwork, I was able to make it to about 80% of my "emergencies."

Such was life in Kijabe - stable and satisfying. But Dr. Barnett, my mentor, friend, and visionary, challenged me with his thoughts about medical needs that remained unmet. I began experiencing an increasing desire to explore these new surgical possibilities, a feeling I called "surgical wanderlust." This led me to expand my skills to help more people, many who would never find help otherwise. Eventually my panorama of care grew from general surgery to obstetrics to some plastics to orthopedics. Finally, what I call "rehab surgery" became my passion. And that all began with a visit to a little town called Kajiado.

RICHARD BRANSFORD

CHAPTER 4

Encountering the Disabled
(1982 – 1988)

"And great crowds came to him, bringing with them the lame, the blind, the crippled, the mute, and many others, and they put them at his feet, and he healed them, so that the crowd wondered, when they saw the mute speaking, the crippled healthy, the lame walking, and the blind seeing. And they glorified the God of Israel."

– Matthew 15: 30, 31

It was not Bethlehem. For me, Kajiado was the birthplace of a new work with disabled children. And, in a strange way, I believe God had been orchestrating this since I was 14, if not before. I had felt fulfilled in many ways before this time, but now I seemed to perceive a greater purpose for my life. When I left Kenya more than three decades later, I felt a strange contentment that many seeds had been planted, a lot of lives had been changed, and a solution had commenced that could help meet many of the needs of the disabled throughout Africa.

In 1982 Millie and I visited the African Inland Church (AIC) Child Care Center in Kajiado, Kenya, a small town located two hours from Kijabe on a road running southeast out of Nairobi toward the Tanzanian border. Giraffe, zebra, impala, Grant's gazelles, and Thomson's gazelles are frequently seen on this broad African plain.

For two years (1977-1978), drought struck these grasslands. The Maasai, a nomadic people that move throughout much of

Kenya and Tanzania to graze and water their livestock, were deeply affected, since the blood and milk of their animals had been their primary source of food for generations. The drought decimated their herds and the resulting famine was catastrophic, especially for a traditionally proud people.

The African Medical and Research Foundation[29] (AM-REF), a.k.a. Flying Doctors, donated food to Lorna Eglund and Betty Alcock, two AIM missionaries working in the area, to distribute to the Massai. Traveling around Maasai land was almost impossible. Few access roads existed and the population was widely scattered. So Lorna and Betty invited the Maasai to come to a temporary feeding center they established in Kajiado. They also encouraged parents to allow their children to stay in the center's dormitories for the duration of the drought so they could receive regular meals and medical care.

Along with the malnourished came children who were disabled. Betty and Lorna noticed that some of the children had paralyzed extremities, most likely due to polio that had struck the region earlier in the '70s.

In this part of the world, the disabled are often believed to be "cursed." They bring shame upon their family, their village, and their country. They are sometimes kept hidden in small rooms or closets or isolated in other ways from the community and not seen by anyone outside their family until they are almost ten years old. And, of course, these children usually have had little or no medical care and, most assuredly, no education.

After the drought subsided, the Maasai parents arrived to collect their children. Knowing how marginalized the disabled were in African culture, Lorna and Betty had real concerns that the disabled children would continue to suffer when they

29 http://www.flydoc.org/

left the center. So they invited them to stay. Those children who could ambulate 50 yards could attend the adjacent primary school and get a formal education, although, among the

Betty Alcock and child at Kajiado, approximately 1982

Maasai, education was not a valued commodity. Learning to herd cows and goats, as well as prepare food and have babies, was what they considered valuable. Because disabled children would be unable to help their families in those ways, their parents appreciated Lorna and Betty's offer and agreed to allow their children to stay in Kajiado. The feeding center became the Kajiado Child Care Center (KCCC).

Lorna and Betty knew they would need more help because neither of them had any real medical background. Providentially, in 1980 they met a Scottish nurse-midwife named

Georgie Orme.[30] Georgie had been forced to leave Uganda during the dictatorship of Idi Amin and didn't know what the Lord wanted her to do next. She went to Mombasa to get a vehicle that her mother had shipped to her, and Lorna and Betty "happened" to be on holiday in Mombasa at that time. Although Georgie told them she "didn't like children" and didn't know anything about rehabilitation of the disabled, they nevertheless invited her to visit Kajiado. Her brief visit became a long-term assignment.

Georgie soon realized that many of the children would benefit from surgery. So she took them to various government and private hospitals, anywhere that she thought she might find help. She didn't always have an appointment, but would sit in operating theater waiting rooms with her kids, hoping a doctor would stop to inquire about them. Sometimes she would sit there the entire day without having any constructive interaction with any medical personnel.

I don't recall the original purpose of why Millie and I went to Kajiado in 1982, but that was when we met Georgie. She kindly served us tea and Scottish shortbread while telling us about the work. We talked and looked at the many Maasai artifacts that lay around the room. With the social formalities over, Georgie suggested that we take a tour. We went to the kitchen and then on to the clinic area and brace shop. Finally we opened the door into the pre-school classroom. Crutches lay scattered across the floor and dozens of children with leg braces filled the room. Before our eyes were Maasai children who had not been immunized against polio. They were the tragic victims of a disease that had been vanquished in most of the West.

30 Orme, G., & Howat, I. (2008). *In Strength Not Our Own: A Maasai Medical Miracle.* Fearn, Ross-shire, Scotland: Christian Focus.

Georgie Orme and children at Kajiado

Most Kenyans, even children, extend their hand in greeting. But the Massai children bowed their heads, anticipating
my touch on the front of their heads. This was unique. Was my
touch a kind of blessing? I think so, but I am not sure. I know
that it was a blessing to me to have these diminutive children
greet me this way. They immediately captured my heart and it
almost felt as if a covenant – a promise – formed between us
during those first few moments.

Personally I had had almost no experience with polio except for those March of Dimes campaigns and the administration of the vaccine in the '50s when I was growing up in California. Back then polio had been real. But it had never quite been this real. Magnifying the impact of that visit to the KCCC classroom was the realization that our twins were the same age as many of those children. Jon and Susie had been immunized against polio in their first year of life. They were among the privileged of the world.

I wonder if Georgie ever really knew the impact that experience in that classroom had on me. Now, years later, the memory is still very fresh in my mind. Perhaps for me this was my personal version of Jacob wrestling with God.[31] That is probably too dramatic, but whatever God was doing in that room that morning was no accident. My hip was not dislocated when I left the room, but the direction of my life surely was. I knew that I was leaving my comfort zone.

"Can you help us?" Georgie asked.

She explained that many of the children needed surgical procedures. She had previously taken them to Kenyatta National Hospital, Nairobi Hospital, the hospital at Lake Magadi, Kikuyu Hospital, and elsewhere. Often she was told there were simply "no beds for her children." Could we help? Could I help?

I have often commented that surgeons are proud people who do not like to say that they don't know how to do a particular operation. I had never seen an operation on a patient with polio. In fact, I don't think that I had ever even read any medical literature about polio. But that sense of "covenant" had settled gently upon my heart. I told Georgie that I would try.

As I've mentioned before, those of us who work in the

31 Genesis 32: 24,25

developing world often perform outside our area of trained expertise, outside our comfort zone. Our patients frequently have no other options available, affordable, or accessible. We may be the end of the line, the last stop. I usually told the families of disabled children that I was not an orthopedist, a neurosurgeon, or a plastic surgeon, or whatever, and explained to them that if they could locate such a specialist they might obtain better care. There have also been times when I have recommended that an operation should be delayed until a visiting specialist could perform it instead of me. At least 90% of the parents have chosen to accept the care that I have been able to provide. Whether this was trust, financial limitations, or ignorance, I don't know.

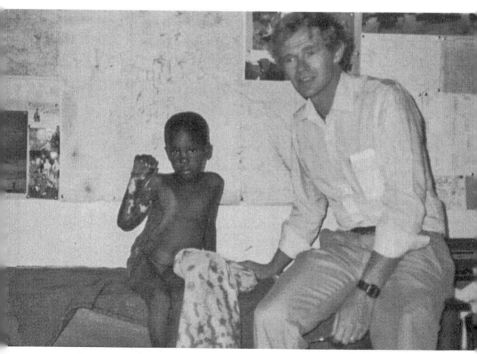

Dick with child with burn contracture at Kajiado

I have always sought to be honest with parents. When complications occurred, or results were not as good as expected, I openly admitted it. But I was always seeking new opportunities to develop my surgical expertise in order to meet the special needs of disabled children. If I was to be the only

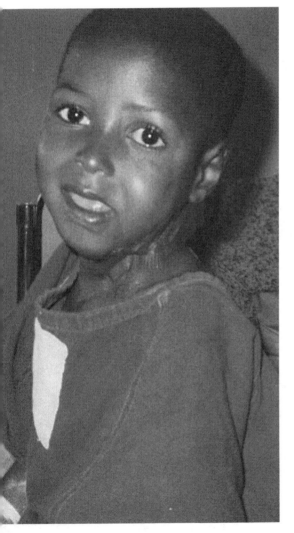

option for some patients, I wanted to be as skilled as I could be and give them the best care I could. Some questioned this approach, but we were in a unique place at a unique time in history. I began making periodic clinic visits to Kajiado. Sometimes I piled more than a few children into my Land Rover and brought them back to Kijabe for their operations - kids with polio, burn contractures[32], club feet[33], amputations,

32 Scar tissue that may prevent to full range of motion of joints, or may distort the normal contour of tissue.
33 A congenital deformity in which one or both feet appear to have been rotated internally at the ankle, causing sufferers to walk on their ankles or on the sides of their feet.

Nashurua, 1984 (opposite page)
and 2014 (right)

and many other problems.

The World Health Organization published a book describing "simple" operations for contractures that occurred secondary to polio. I started doing some of these operations, but honestly, they were not as simple as described. Not all operations went perfectly, but most children were helped. We visited Kajiado every four to six weeks and continued doing so for over ten years.

During one of my early visits, I met Nashurua. She was four or five years old at the time and had burn contractures of her neck, chest, left arm, and hand. For me there was something very special about this little girl. Maybe it was because she was nearly the age of my twins. I wanted to help her so much, but at this point in my surgical career I had not had any significant training in plastic surgery.

Nashurua could not look straight ahead because of the burn contracture on her neck, so I first released that by taking flaps of skin from her chest and transferring them to her neck. I skin-grafted her chest where the transferred flaps had originally been. Later we did operations on her left hand and arm to improve their function and appearance.

During her visits to Kijabe, Nashurua learned to cross the field from the hospital and find her way to our home, often arriving completely unannounced. We would invite her in and she would make herself at home, playing with Jon and Susie's toys. When it was time for dinner, it was natural for her to stay and eat with us. (We telephoned the pediatric ward to inform them that she was at our home.) After dinner, she seemed to think that it was just her right to crawl into my lap for our devotional time when we would read about God and Jesus from a book with pictures. At this time I think that Nashurua knew fewer than ten English words. Sometimes our twins looked on somewhat jealously at this little intruder sitting in their father's lap. After devotions one of us would walk her back to the hospital where she often awaited an operation the following day.

Our family was to return to the U.S. for a year in July 1988. On a visit to Kajiado early that year, Nashurua, then possibly ten years old, approached me with a going away gift - a beautiful beaded Maasai belt. Utilizing her very, very limited English vocabulary, she expressed a simple thank you from the whole center. Tears came to my eyes and I haltingly expressed my words of appreciation with a huge lump in my throat.

By 2010, KCCC director Daniel Sapayia[34] wrote to tell me that Kajiado had "fallen on hard times." The financial crisis that had affected much of the world had also impacted them. My friend and assistant, David Ng'ang'a, and I drove to Kajiado one morning. It seemed that the center was slower than it had once been. Daniel and I talked, and I examined many of their reports. I saw no significant improprieties, but I did understand that an impending financial crisis could close the center. (Fortunately the center has remained open.)

34 See profile in Appendix.

Before we visited, I asked Daniel if Nashurua was living nearby. He told me that she was. She came to see me while we were there. By then she was a very quiet 32-year-old mother of three. She was poor, desperately poor. I had suspicions that her marriage was not good. We sat together and there were some rather long periods of silence. Though scarred in body and not very wise in many ways, she was kind and radiated love. She gave me the impression that she just wanted to be there and enjoy the memories of the past.

In 2014, Nashurua stopped by the center again, wearing a magnificent beaded Maasai necklace, a colorful shawl, and a big smile. Her eyes sparkled and her voice was soft as she remembered her childhood walks up the hill in Kijabe to spend her evenings with the Bransford family. In some ways she hadn't changed a bit. This was the little girl that I loved and still care for. She will always be very special to me.

SALA[35]

In November 1994, a staff member from World Vision[36], a Christian humanitarian organization dedicated to improving the lives of children around the globe, came to Kijabe bringing a strange letter. The essence of the letter was, "Would you please operate on Sala?" Sala was a twelve-year-old girl with the secondary effects of polio affecting both legs. She had not walked since she was an infant. She was from the Wolof tribal group and lived in an isolated village in Senegal, approximately 4,000 miles away. I personally felt that the request for help was impractical and unnecessary.

35 Some information for this profile was taken from an article published in the May, 1996, issue of the *Kijabe Mirror*, a Kijabe Hospital publication, and from an article by Lois Ephraim entitled "Walking Tall" in the Autumn 1998 edition of *World Vision News*.
36 http://www.worldvision.org

I responded to the letter and suggested that a closer site would be a better option, but no closer site could be found. Then I commented that I did not know enough about Sala to be sure that she would improve with operations. Photos were sent with a description of the physical findings. From those I was able to determine that surgical releases of the contractures (shortening and hardening of muscles, tendons, or other tissue), plus braces, would probably allow her to walk with crutches.

But why Kijabe?

As the story unfolded, Miss Lois Ephraim, an employee of Russ Reid Company, had been hired by World Vision to help present the work they were doing and the needs in Senegal. She met Sala in 1992 during her first visit to Africa. The shy nine-year-old girl could only crawl on blistered hands and knees. Her twisted legs flopped back and forth in the hot, desert sand. She became crippled at 18 months by paralytic poliomyelitis - a virus that could have been prevented with two drops of polio vaccine. Confined to the family's circle of huts, Sala couldn't play with other children, participate in village activities, or attend school. Her parents said she was a "stranger" in the community.

When they said their goodbyes that day, Sala's mother, Mbaytou, grabbed Lois's hand and whispered, "Please help my Sala."

Lois had no idea how to arrange orthopedic surgery for Sala in Africa. But the Lord knew. Sometime after meeting Sala, Lois' mother had a stroke. When Lois returned to Chicago to help her mother during rehab, she met Dr. Bill Adair, her mother's rehab doctor. She remembered Sala and asked Dr. Adair where Sala might find help. He commented that Shriners Hospital in Chicago was an option, but suggested that Sala be taken to Kijabe Hospital where he had worked for a year.

When arrangements had been made for Sala and her father to come to Kijabe, I did a little research on the Wolof tribe. I was told that it is primarily Muslim and a part of an "unreached people group," a population that had never heard the Gospel of Jesus Christ. I visited the Gospel Recordings office in Nairobi and asked the clerk if they had anything in the Wolof language. He appeared confused and quickly said, "I don't think so." However, he consulted some books and found there were portions of the Gospels recorded in Wolof. I bought tapes of the New Testament and a crank-type tape recorder. During their upcoming visit, Sala's father would hear the Gospel through these tapes.

So they came to Kijabe in 1996 and Sala had bilateral hip and knee releases (corrections of the tissue contractures). After the operation she remained in a spica cast[37] for approximately one month. She was then fitted with bilateral long leg braces, metal supports on both legs to provide stability and strength. She began to walk, first with a walker and later with crutches. She was hospitalized for approximately two months. Once a week the only Wolof-speaking family in Nairobi came to Kijabe to translate for the medical team. When Sala left the hospital she returned to Senegal. Eventually, she received better braces from the U.S.

In 1998, Lois returned to Senegal to see Sala. As they drove into the village, she spotted a tall teenage girl in a bright red and white dress among the throng of welcomers. She jumped out of the vehicle and headed for her. Smiling, Sala picked up her crutches and walked toward Lois - strong and confident, swinging her metal leg braces. They hugged tearfully as the villagers clapped and chanted. Sala unfolded

37 A spica cast (also called a hip spica cast or body cast) immobilizes the hips, thighs, and knees so that bones or tendons can heal properly.

83

a piece of paper and sang a song she had written - a traditional way of honoring a special guest in Africa.

"Al hamdoulilah," said Sala's father, Moussa, greeting her with the Muslim expression meaning "praise be to God." "I cannot repay you for what you have done for my daughter. But God will pay you for us." He spoke in Wolof, his native language, via a translator. But the joy in his eyes needed no interpretation.

Sala was making up for lost time. She was the top student in the local literacy classes. She wanted to be a seamstress and run her own business. Once a stranger to the people in her village, she was now the most popular girl in the community.

"We never thought Sala would walk," said her mother, Mbaytou, as they celebrated over a traditional meal of yassa poulet, a spicy dish of chicken and onions. "Now we know nothing is impossible."

I thank God for bringing Sala to us. Please continue to pray for her. Who knows what two months in a Christian hospital and hearing the Gospel in their native Wolof language will do? Were seeds planted? God knows.

CHAPTER 5

Learning from Doctors God Sent My Way (1980 – 1991)

"So he departed from there and found Elisha the son of Shaphat, who was plowing with twelve yoke of oxen in front of him, and he was with the twelfth. Elijah passed by him and cast his cloak upon him. And he left the oxen and ran after Elijah and said, "Let me kiss my father and my mother, and then I will follow you." And he said to him, "Go back again, for what have I done to you?" And he returned from following him and took the yoke of oxen and sacrificed them and boiled their flesh with the yokes of the oxen and gave it to the people, and they ate. Then he arose and went after Elijah and assisted him." I Kings 19:19-21

During the various periods of my life God seemed to send "Elijahs" to me. Maybe I should call these people Dr. Elijahs: Dr. Bill Barnett, Dr. Ted Williams, Dr. Joe Stiles, Dr. Stan Topple, Dr. Greg Hellwarth, Dr. Louis Carter, and many others. Some would call them mentors, but my Elijahs were more to me than that. They taught me stepping stone skills that equipped me to perform surgeries I probably would not have attempted without their guidance. Did our paths cross by coincidence? No, there are no coincidences for the children of God. The God who orchestrated me from conception and a single cell, to a mature fetus, to birth and life chooses to walk with me and send Elijahs and angels to work in and through me, bringing honor and glory to Himself.

As a kid I used to play with a building set called Tinker Toys. Many different pieces could be fitted together into magnificent structures, but often I had to envision the end product early in the process. Seldom did anything good come out of random action. Likewise, God always had an end product in His mind for His work in me.

During the 1980s and '90s, many pieces were coming together to be assembled into the structure God had in mind for our family's life and work in Africa. But that structure was hard to see and interpret at the beginning, and it ultimately depended, at least in part, on my perspective about God's role in bringing the good into the lives of His children at the right time and in the right way. I believe that the world came into existence immediately and completely at the divine word of a Master Designer. This makes it easier for me to discern His design in my own life.

Through the lens of time, I now see clouds of related events. I'm presenting them this way to clarify how the events of my life seemed to fit together in His plan. I was very content with this exercise, for the seemingly unrelated events that spread over the years decreased in perceived randomness and became more characteristic of design. Frequently we only see the back of our life's tapestry where threads resemble a tangled mess rather than looking at the front where the Designer exhibits His amazing artistry.

Our family in Kijabe grew in happy busy-ness during these years as we hosted scores of medical students and volunteers. Many lived in our home with our family or in our guest quarters, two small rooms located behind our house. Our homestead could accommodate a total of 16 at one time. The young people who came were generally a delight and made us laugh with their fun-loving pranks. Our children became so accustomed to having visitors at the table that they would wilt with disappointment if we told them that there wouldn't be a guest for dinner.

As our kids matured, they added variety to our after-dinner family devotions. New types of prayer were initiated: fishermen prayers, wise men prayers, pop up prayers, short prayers, sentence prayers, pick-up prayers, and a variety of other types.[38] Some endured and others faded into vague memories. We laughed a lot and enjoyed the Lord.

Our family functioned well as a team. If we worked well together, life could be fun and productive. But if each one did not play his or her part, our seemingly calm home could become chaotic. Each Saturday morning, Millie and I would make a list of chores for our kids. Chris, the oldest, was usually the one entrusted to assign appropriate tasks for everyone. There is a nine-year gap in age from Chris to the twins, plus a corresponding gap in maturity. We did have the occasional complaint, but there were not too many because the one who complained had to trade jobs with Chris! The chores included cooking (especially desserts), tidying up the living room, cleaning one's bedroom, washing windows, feeding the animals (lovebirds[39], dikdiks[40], and many rabbits), washing the car inside and out, and dumping the trash in the pit. Everyone tried to make doing these things as much fun as possible.

God was also assembling a team of Elijahs for me, sending them regularly into my life to help prepare me for my work with the disabled. Dr. Bill Barnett and the Kajiado trip had already piqued my interest in the work with the disabled. Now

---

38 See Appendix for explanations.
39 Small parrot species indigenous to Africa that exhibits strong monogamous pair bonding.
40 Small antelope that lives in the bush lands of eastern and southern Africa.

other doctors began coming to help with the germinating effort.

Dr. Ted Willliams spent 35 years in the West Nile district of Uganda working as a missionary doctor. Ted wasn't just a surgeon - he was an "everything." He had to be, for he was working solo much of the time. He continued working in Uganda through Idi Amin, the tyrant dictator. Dr. Williams left that country only when he fractured his hip. Dr. Bill pinned his hip at Kijabe. During his recovery, Ted saw the extent of the need and potential at Kijabe.

After fully recovering, Ted and his wife Muriel returned to Uganda. But when they retired in 1979, they returned to Kijabe because their daughter, son-in-law, and grandchildren lived there. Ted and Muriel were wonderful, warm people. Ted had a great sense of humor. He also had a deep interest in cancer, and especially Burkitt's lymphoma.[41] In fact, Dr. Dennis Burkitt, after whom the lymphoma was named, was one of Ted's very special friends. They were companions on a historical trip from Uganda to South Africa surveying geographical locations where Burkitt's lymphoma occurred.

Ted became like a father to me during his brief years at Kijabe. He too was a dreamer. He wondered if perhaps there could be a medical school at Kijabe. He started the cancer registry to record details about each cancer patient as a means to better understand the disease in an African setting. He developed our skin test for hydatid cyst.[42] He was a humble teacher. I regret that he did not remain longer to advise me about how to better develop the work with the disabled. However he felt

---

41 A rapidly growing and often fatal form of non-Hodgkin's cancer that starts in immune cells called B-cells.
42 Parasitic disease of tapeworms that is often asymptomatic, making it difficult to detect and diagnose.

that it was time for him to return to England and establish a home and identity there.

In 1980, Dr. Joe Stiles, a fully trained orthopedic surgeon, came to Kijabe for one month. He was not only a skilled orthopedist, but also a kind and patient teacher. His past experience had included the surgical care of polio victims in the U.S. when it was still an epidemic there. He was at Kijabe when the early waves of polio victims were arriving for surgery. He returned to Kijabe every year for 15 years, staying three to six months each time, and even came periodically after his stateside retirement in 1991.

Joe and Nancy once lived in our home for a few months while our family was in the U.S. Their stay included graciously watching after our pesky dog Sawyer. Sawyer had the unwise habit of chasing motorcycles, and one day one of them got the best of him. Joe was such a caring orthopedist that he even took good care of the broken leg of our dog. When we returned, thanks to Joe's care and Nancy's good bedside manner, Sawyer already had his cast off, and (unfortunately) was back chasing motorcycles again!

A much younger mentor, encourager, and friend was Dr. Greg Hellwarth, an orthopedist and spine surgeon. Greg was smart and well prepared to tackle most cases, especially if a patient had no other alternatives. I believe that Greg visited Kijabe over 15 times, eventually also accompanying me to other countries.

In 1982, a new challenge presented itself. A somewhat crackling voice came across the shortwave radio from Gatab[43] in the Northern Frontier of Kenya asking if we could put in

---

43 Gatab is on Mt. Kulal and situated among the Rendille people. This is where I helped build a road in 1966.

a shunt[44] for a child with hydrocephalus. There was no one at Kenyatta National Hospital available to do this at that time. I said that I didn't think we had anyone at Kijabe who had ever done this operation. I had never seen the procedure. But I returned to the hospital and asked the only other surgeon about his experience inserting shunts for hydrocephalus. He told me that he had never seen one inserted. That seemed to confirm that neither of us could do this procedure with any level of safety; plus we didn't even have a shunt.

About two weeks later, a letter arrived from a Chinese neurosurgeon practicing in Los Angeles. I had no idea how he got my name. The letter said, "I am coming to Kenya on a safari; could I have a tour of your hospital?" It seemed amazingly providential. I first determined that the child in Gatab still needed a shunt, and then I called my brother, Jack, who lived in the Los Angeles area. I asked him to contact the neurosurgeon and tell him that we would be delighted to give him a tour, and, by the way, how would he like to insert a shunt? And could he bring the shunt along with him? The surgeon agreed and within a few weeks he flew to Kenya.

Knowing his arrival date, we arranged for the child to be brought to Kijabe Hospital. The surgeon arrived at the hospital at 8:00 a.m. and was scrubbed and in the operating room by 8:30 a.m. By 9:30 the operation was completed. He only inserted one shunt, but he brought two. He left the unused one for future use. We gave him a hospital tour. He left. We never heard from him again.

Was he an angel? I don't know, but I do know that his visit opened a new chapter in the life of our hospital, and an even

44 A ventriculoperitoneal shunt is designed to shunt cerebrospinal fluid under pressure from the dilated ventricles of the brain to the abdominal cavity with a one way, pressure-sensitive valve that controls the direction and quantity of flow.

bigger chapter in my personal and professional life. That was the beginning of our work with children with hydrocephalus. That was the only shunt I saw inserted by a professional until approximately 2000. In spite of this lack of expertise, we inserted a growing number of shunts and revised the technique as time progressed.

We soon realized we would need more shunts. Supplies are always an issue for any mission hospital. Dr. Paul Baumann was a radiotherapist working in Wichita, Kansas. He collected outdated or unused items that his hospital was discarding. He sorted these items and sent many of them to Kijabe through the mail. Several months later, sometimes as long as a year, they would arrive at the door of the hospital. Often these boxes included items that we had wished for but never expected to have. For some unknown reason, I was usually the one who unpacked these boxes. One day not long after that first shunt operation, near the bottom of one of the boxes, I discovered seven boxes labeled "SHUNTS." I was so surprised and wondered, Did an angel sneak those into that box?

I eventually used all of those shunts, those "angel gifts." For several years, we put in fewer than four shunts per year. I could beg this small number from neurosurgical friends and other doctors. But eventually we needed more and I began looking for other sources. Dr. Mel Cheatham[45], a neurosurgeon in California, was especially kind to us and supplied most of the early shunts. He had been to Tenwek Hospital in Bomet, Kenya, and understood our need better than others who had never been to Africa.

I continued to visit other locations in Kenya to expand our medical outreach and spiritual opportunities. From 1984

45 Cheatham, Mel (2004). *Make a Difference.* Nashville, Tennessee: W Publishing Group (a division of Thomas Nelson Publishers)

through 1994, Keith Weaver (a friend with no formal medical training but who watched over the patients at Kijabe Hospital during anesthesia) and I flew regularly to Lamu, an island off the northeastern coast of Kenya. The town on the island dates back to the 1400s and is the oldest continually occupied town in Kenya. It was settled by Muslim Arab and Indian traders, who came with their merchandise and their people in large boats called dhows (traditional vessels with large triangular sails used in the Indian Ocean). Some intermarried with the local people. Their Muslim faith became mingled with traditional tribal beliefs, resulting in what is sometimes referred to as "folk Islam." This was, and is, the dominant religion on this part of the Kenyan coast.

The old hospital was small, as was the operating room. A single overhead fluorescent bulb and a gooseneck lamp with a 25-watt bulb provided the only available light in the OR. During our introductory visit we asked the hospital doctors if they were interested in having surgical help on a periodic basis. They were very welcoming, so we sought permission from the Ministry of Health, which gave its official approval.

During our first working visit, I made rounds along with the two government doctors, deciding together which patients would be good candidates for safe surgery there. We went from bed to bed with relatively routine presentations of the medical histories of each patient. Finally we came to the bed of a teenage girl for whom a translator was requested. Nearly everyone spoke Swahili in the Lamu area, so I asked why we needed a translator. I was told that the young lady was from a hunter and gatherer tribe (unnamed for security reasons) of about 3,500 to 5,000 people. I felt a tingle of joy and excitement. At that time there were no known Christians among this tribe. The young lady had an infection in her knee that did not necessitate an operation, but she did need a brace to help prevent a contracture. We dutifully measured her for a brace to be made at Kajiado.

When we returned on our next trip, we delivered the brace to her in her home village. She agreed to accompany us to other very isolated villages of her people where we saw more disabled children. Our supporters prayed for this tribe in response to our visit. One of the possible fruits is that now, decades later, there are a few believers among this people group.

Keith and I made bi-monthly visits to the Lamu District Hospital, staying four or five days each time. We often took an assortment of medical supplies, braces, and special shoes. Sometimes visitors would accompany us on those trips. Normally, however, we were a team of two, sharing a variety of responsibilities and plenty of laughs. We did prostatectomies (removal of the prostate gland), hernia repairs, vesicovaginal fistulas[46], skin grafts, Caesarian sections, as well as clubfoot corrections, release of contractures due to polio and burns, genu varus and valgus[47], and many other cases. Some of these procedures had never been done in Lamu.

Some of the polio deformities were new to me, and I had difficulty finding examples in major orthopedic books. It was humbling and very challenging. We improvised a lot, but we had some very thankful young patients when we were finished.

On one occasion, we went by boat to nearby islands, Faza and Pate, to see patients. We would occasionally have to re-

---

46 An abnormal opening between the urinary bladder and the vagina resulting in the leakage of urine, usually secondary to trauma while giving birth.
47 Referring to the knee, i.e. varus-slang: bow-legged; a knee deformity with the knee turned inward to an abnormal degree; valgus (slang): knock-kneed; a deformity in which the knee is turned outward to an abnormal degree.

fer surgical candidates back to Lamu. On two occasions, we traveled by helicopter to other very remote sites, one of these being to a tiny village inhabited by the previously mentioned tribe. We visited Kiunga on the Somalia border, Ndau Island, and other sites. Our reputation for compassion and quality care often preceded us, and as a result, locals would welcome us like old friends in places we had never previously visited.

In the town of Lamu, some of my closest friends were Gujarati Indians who had been there for generations. One was Shabir, who befriended me and accompanied me into the homes of many sick people in the community and on some of the helicopter trips. On one occasion I entered a small home and heard an older lady muttering on the other side of a small curtain. I did not know the language, but my curiosity was aroused. I asked her daughter if her mother was talking to someone, and she nonchalantly replied, "Satan." I was shocked. I examined her and prescribed some medicine. At the end of our visit, I asked the old lady if I could pray for her. She agreed and I prayed in Jesus' name.

I enjoyed many evenings in Shabir's home. He often invited my companions and me to a banquet at his house. His wife prepared wonderful Indian food and his children helped serve the feast. We did not use knives, forks or spoons for these meals, only hands – more specifically, the right hand. The left hand is the "dirty hand" in this culture. So I learned to eat with my right hand, pushing food into my mouth with my thumb. When left-handed people accompanied me, I reminded them repeatedly about the need to use their right hands. On these visits I often examined Shabir's mother, wife, friends and neighbors and attempted to treat them. He and his brother came to Kijabe on one occasion, and I removed one of his brother's kidneys because it was cancerous. He survived and did well for several years. I watched Shabir's children grow up. His oldest son went to Russia to train to be a doctor. His youngest, a daughter, went to school to be a lawyer.

In 1990, during RVA's April vacation, my daughter Bethany and I decided to visit Joytown.[48] I had heard about it and wanted to visit there for some time. Joytown was a special school for the disabled located in the town of Thika, about two hours from Kijabe. There were over 400 disabled children there, attending two schools: a primary school and secondary school.

We arrived shortly before lunch and stationed ourselves on a bench opposite the cafeteria. When a school bell rang, children with decrepit wheelchairs, crutches, braces, and walkers, poured out of their classrooms. Most of them wore torn clothing. Some of them were wet with urine. Some had polio. Others had club feet, cerebral palsy, and amputations. Watching them make their way into the dining room, I leaned over and whispered to Bethany, "We could improve the quality of life for probably 85% of these kids!"

And that was how our work began at Joytown. I spoke with the headmaster. We set a date to return to evaluate the physical needs of his children. Within a year of beginning our work at Joytown, the headmaster at Joytown suggested that we visit Joyland Primary School for the Disabled in Kisumu, which is on the banks of Lake Victoria.[49] In 1991, Caroline, a Kenyan physical therapist assigned to Joyland, asked me to visit the school in Kisumu and evaluate the students there. I encouraged two of our visiting American physical therapists to go and screen the children first. One was a short-term worker

---

48 http://web.salvationarmy.org/kya/www_kya.nsf/vwsublinks/0a7653ace6324d808025755300 1b6f7d?opendocument. See also profile for David Ng'ang'a in Appendix.
49 http://www.salvationarmy.org.au/en/get-involved/sponsor-a-child/Newsletter/Joyland-Secondary-Special-School-Kenya/

at Kapsowar and one was assigned to Kijabe for a year. They agreed to do this, met at Joyland, and reviewed the children with Caroline, who had a fantastic knowledge of each child's medical history and progress. They spent two full days reviewing patients.

I arrived on the third day, examined approximately 50 of

Dick and Joytown kids

the children, and suggested operations for many of them. The staff at the school communicated with those parents and 14 children were chosen to be the first from Joyland to come to Kijabe for their operations. A local Rotary Club provided funds for transport and other needs. We made special arrangements with the Kenya Railway authorities to bring them to Kijabe by train.

The children left Kisumu one afternoon and were scheduled to arrive at Kijabe Town Station the next day at around 5 AM. The Kijabe Town Station was not a safe place to be at that time of the morning, however, one of our staff took our Volkswagen bus to the station to meet Caroline and the children.

The task of getting the children off the train was tricky. The train was scheduled to stop for only a few minutes. Most of the children had polio and needed help to disembark. Despite this concern, all went well and they arrived at the hospital early that morning.

We admitted and examined them, did lab work, and over a period of three days, completed all of their operations. All had casts on at least one leg. Some had casts on both. All had been measured for braces before their operations. Most of those braces were made in the week and a half that they remained at Kijabe Hospital.

The day of departure came and they were to leave from the Matathia Train Station at about 7:30 PM. We drove two vans filled with anxious adults and happy, chattering kids in casts and braces. As our vehicles climbed a rather steep hill about a mile before the train station, we encountered a truck on its side, blocking the road. We were forced to take a longer way to the station. Fortunately, we got there before the train arrived. We told the stationmaster about our "mission" and asked where the railroad car on which the children would be boarding might stop. The location was identified and we parked the two vans near that spot.

The luggage was arranged, the braces were assembled, the kids were ready - or at least we thought we were ready. Everyone was cautiously excited. As the train came into view, we prepared ourselves for the brief three-minute stop during which we had to get all of the children and their luggage on the train.

To our dismay, the designated train car stopped about 30 yards farther up the track! Caroline started running with one child in her arms. She boarded the train, sat that child on the floor, and reached for the next, moving each one away from the entry area as she lifted them aboard. The rest of us hastily ran back and forth, panting and carrying laughing children.

Then the whistle blew, signaling that the train was leaving. We still had three children left to board! Rob, one of the medical students, hustled down the tracks, jumped on the train, and helped pull the final few children on. Only when the train began to roll did Rob swing down. We stood beside the tracks laughing and catching our breath while we waved goodbye to Caroline and the children. Mission accomplished!

It has been 25 years since that first visit to Joytown, and the work has not only continued but also improved. Literally hundreds of operations have been done for the children there and from other similar facilities. In addition, eventually the medical work on Lamu was transferred to a new hospital built by Saudi Arabia, which was a major step up from the old facility. Progress in that area has been made also, but this has not been easy.

All of these people, places, and events were an integral part of God's plan. Although there were still many weaknesses in our work with the disabled, the evolving effort was beginning to make more sense and reveal more evidence of His blessing and design.

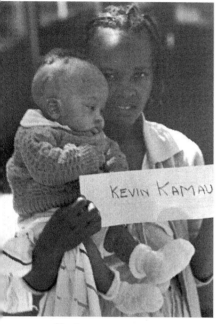

Kevin

KEVIN

There are children I've treated whom I'll always remember. Kevin was one of those.

One afternoon in 1990 Kevin and his mother found their way to Kijabe Hospital. They lived in Nairobi where they had been attending the Kenyatta National Hospital Neurosurgical Clinic; they had been waiting several months to have the cystic swelling on his back repaired. When Kevin was about six months old she brought him to Kijabe having heard that we were providing care for disabled children.

At that time only a few cases of spina bifida (a birth defect where there is incomplete closure of the backbone, membranes, and the spinal cord) had come for care. Dr. Bob Bowers had repaired most of these. I took Kevin to see Bob, and he agreed to close the defect. However, he had no time to do the operation until the following week. Kevin's mother agreed to return then.

The day before she was scheduled to return she arrived with Kevin. She was anxious because the cystic swelling had ruptured and fluid was draining from his back. We cleaned and dressed the wound, put Kevin on antibiotics, and prepared him for surgery the following morning. The closure went well, and he remained in the hospital for a few days allowing us to determine if he would develop secondary hydrocephalus, a condition that occurs when fluid builds up in the skull, causing swelling in the brain and subsequent brain damage.

As expected, the ventricles, fluid-filled cavities in the center of the brain, enlarged. I inserted a Chhabra shunt into his brain. This is a device with a one-way valve that channels brain fluid to the peritoneum (membrane of the abdominal cavity) where it can be reabsorbed. All seemed to be fine and Kevin was discharged a few days later. From that point on, I saw him and his mother regularly. His head size stabilized and his back seemed to heal nicely. Kevin's lower extremities were partially paralyzed, but he eventually was able to walk with braces and crutches. He had no control of his bladder or bowels. Kevin's mother was faithful and careful to do clean intermittent catheterization (CIC)[50] and care for his other needs.

In January 1993, Kevin's mother returned to the clinic. She reported that she didn't think that Kevin was as mentally alert as he had been the previous month. I suggested that it would be best if she sought the advice of a real neurosurgeon in Nairobi, because I did not really think that I was the best choice for his care at that point.

Kevin was taken to Nairobi where a CT scan was done. It suggested to the neurosurgeon that the shunt was probably

---

50 Clean intermittent catheterization is the temporary placement of a catheter (tube) to remove urine when the muscles of the bladder are damaged or weakened. Clean refers to careful handwashing and sanitary techniques to avoid infection.

disconnected. He chose to insert a new shunt on the left side of the head. Unfortunately, after this operation an infection developed. His mother was unable to pay additional neurosurgical fees and returned to Kijabe. Recognizing the infection, I removed the new shunt. After the infection on the left resolved, I chose to re-explore the shunt on the right. I found this shunt to be working very adequately. I really could not, and still cannot, explain his mother's observations. After exploring the original shunt, the wound broke down, necessitating the removal of that shunt.

I did not know what to do. Via e-mail I consulted friends who were neurosurgeons. Based upon their advice, I chose to place Kevin on Diamox, a diuretic that many do not think has any benefit in reducing intracranial (in the skull) pressure. However, Kevin seemed to stabilize and after about three months the Diamox was stopped without further problems.

Kevin grew. Other than braces and need for help with his bladder and bowels, he did well. He had a wonderful mother who loved him dearly. He was reasonably intelligent. He transferred from a school in Nairobi to Joytown, a school for the disabled, when he was about 10 and seemed to do well there.

I returned to Kenya in December 2003 after being away for five months. I was very sad to learn that while I was away Kevin apparently developed ventriculitis, an infection of the cerebrospinal fluid, and passed away rather quickly.

Kevin was one of the first patients who came to us for spina bifida repair and shunting. Even though he did not live a long life, the operations seemed to improve the quality of his life. During that time he brought a lot of joy to his mother and those who knew him.

ANNIE

To say the least, it was bizarre. Our mobile clinic team went to Joytown Special School to review patients. A new student arrived. Annie, then about eight years old, hesitatingly walked forward. She had specially-crafted shoes, but it was obvious that her feet turned backwards. I extended my hand to greet Annie only to discover that her hands were different too.

I carefully examined this friendly young girl. All of her fingers were webbed and the bones at their tips were fused, much like an American baseball catcher's mitt. This is called complex syndactyly. Her mother also had uncorrected webbed hands. Annie was unable to pull her thumb across to her small finger because those muscles were missing. I then looked at her feet. She had ten toes and two very shortened Achilles tendons on each foot. The latter condition forced her to walk on upper surfaces of her feet, rather than the soles of her feet.

I felt that Annie would need a number of surgical procedures. We would first concentrate on separating Annie's fingers. Only one hand could be operated upon at a time, and each hand needed at least two operations. I don't think that her family realized how many procedures Annie would need.

It was Sunday during one of Annie's early trips to Kijabe. That day I was the preacher at Rift Valley Academy Chapel, addressing approximately 500 people, students ranging in age from kindergarten to 12th grade, plus teachers and family members. I usually focused on merging Scripture with my work among the disabled, sharing the magnitude of the need, and the spiritual and medical opportunities among disabled children. I wanted my audiences to see more of God, but also to realize that our work was a compassionate attempt to be "Jesus in the flesh" to these children and their parents.

It occurred to me that Annie could help me communicate my message. I certainly did not want to embarrass her or put her on display. We had developed a relationship that I didn't want to violate. But I spoke to her quietly about the chapel service and what I hoped to achieve. Her presence would be a message that I could never adequately communicate in words. I asked her if she would consider walking with me to the platform. She seemed to understand and gladly agreed. Her presence had a dramatic effect on some of those in chapel that morning.

All of Annie's fingers were eventually liberated. She was able to write better and to do other tasks more effectively. Another surgeon from another institution operated on her feet, but ultimately she had below-the-knee amputations and was fitted for artificial legs. The last time I saw Annie I had been examining children at Joytown and went across to the dining room where lunch was being served. Annie was about 12 years old at the time and was sitting with her friends. There was an empty place on the bench for me (if I squeezed in a bit). I went over and sat with them. We talked and laughed together. I showed them photos of my family. Our "African son" Joshua (his story is in the next chapter) was a big topic of conversation among those typical pre-teen girls!

Not long after that encounter, Annie left Joytown and I have not been able to locate her.

Annie is an unforgettable memory, not only because she had such unusual congenital deformities, but for the person she was. She smiled, laughed, and went on living. She made

Annie

friends easily. She was thankful, outgoing, and cooperative. She had the unusual skill of being able to make others feel good and seemingly had a great outlook on life in spite of her problems.

God bless Annie, wherever she is.

RICHARD BRANSFORD

CHAPTER 6

Venturing Beyond My Comfort Zone (1992 – 1996)

"I persevered in the work on this wall, and we acquired no land, and all my servants were gathered there for the work."
Nehemiah 5:16

In July 1992, our busy family life was about to get busier. An abandoned baby boy with a fractured skull, hypothermia, and pneumonia was brought to the hospital. He was found on the bank of a stream at an elevation of 9000 ft. with his feet in the water and his head on a rock. The nurses at Kijabe Hospital named him Moses because he had been found in the water. As a consultant, I evaluated his neurological status. It was my opinion that no operation was indicated. Initially, he was not expected to live, but after eight days of medical care, he perked up and became the darling of the nursing staff.

That very month, Millie borrowed a book from the RVA school library entitled *Twelve-Part Harmony*[51]. The book was about the Williams family who had 12 children – four of their own, four adopted Korean children, and four adopted Filipino kids. Millie finished the book while we were at the coast on vacation. She once again prayed for God's clear guidance and again this question was before us. We had talked, dreamed, and prayed about possibly adopting children for many years.

---

51 Williams, Pat, Jill Williams, and Beth Spring. 1990. *Twelve-part Harmony.* Old Tappan, N.J.: F.H. Revell.

We had even investigated agencies that cared for orphans from Romania, Ireland, and Cambodia. It was a bit daunting to think about adopting since she was almost 49 and I was nearing 52. But Millie conceded that if God wanted us to raise another child, He would give us one and we would be ready.

After vacation I went back to the hospital and encountered Baby Moses happily living at the nurses' station. He was adorable, but very distracting to the staff! I called our house to see if perhaps Susie, our daughter, could take him home for the afternoon. We didn't have food for him. We didn't have diapers. But we did have attention to give him. So Moses came to the Bransford home "for the afternoon."

Two weeks later, he was still in our home.

Initially, Millie and I felt a bit old to be up at night with an infant. So to alleviate that, Bethany, Susan, and Jon, who were home at the time, came up with an alternate plan. Bethany would take the nightshift the first night, Susie the second night, Jon the third night, and so on. Jon did not make it through his night, but the girls made up for that. They wanted to make sure this new baby would stay with the Bransford clan.

A visiting pediatrician evaluated him and estimated his age at six months. That was August 5, so we counted back and gave him February 5 as his birthday. After two weeks of having him in our home, we went to the Child Welfare Office in Kiambu to determine if, and how, we might become his legal foster parents. They told us we had to be younger than 45; our youngest child had to be less than five years older than the child to be fostered; and we should be from the same "tribe." We struck out on all counts: we were certainly over 45, our twins were already 15, and we didn't belong to any tribe. Our hearts sank. But God gave us favor with the agency. They allowed us to take him home anyway, although without legal custody. Bethany named him Joshua and kept Moses as his middle name. We made him a part of our family. Informally, that is.

In order to have legal custody we needed a police report from the Lari Police Station expressing the circumstances. This took nine months, but in the end, we were given foster parent status. On February 4, 1995, one day before Joshua's designated third birthday, we appeared before Priscine Judge Effie Owuor at the main court in Nairobi, and Joshua Moses officially became a Bransford.

We believe that God sent Joshua to be a member of our family and "dwell among us." I began pondering that word "dwell" with regard to the work with the disabled. Dwell is a somewhat old-fashioned term. *The New Oxford American Dictionary* has two definitions:

• Live in or at a specified place.

• Think, speak, or write at length about a topic

Neither of these definitions fully satisfies the depth I believe God communicates in Scripture:

I will dwell in the house of the Lord forever (Psalms 23:6).

I long to dwell in your tent forever and take refuge in the shelter of your wings (Psalms 61:4).

I pray that out of his glorious riches he may strengthen you with power through His Spirit in your inner being, so that Christ may dwell in your hearts through faith. And I pray that you, being rooted and established in love, may have power, together with all the saints, to grasp how wide and long and high and deep is the love of Christ, and to know the love that surpasses knowledge---that you may be filled to the measure of all the fullness of God (Ephesians 3: 16-19).

God's idea of dwelling means to be truly at home: settled, contented, and safe.

By 1992, we were looking for a place where the rehabilitation work could develop and expand, a dwelling separate from Kijabe Hospital. Ruth Scott Kelley, a lady who had invested herself in caring for disabled children on her small farm, suggested that we look at the Grant Estate near Molo, a little over three hours northwest of Nairobi. The location, existing buildings, and available land looked very promising. But after a year of negotiating, the purchase failed. I was deeply disappointed. One day I will ask God to help me understand this difficult episode.

At the same time, I realized that the envisioned work with the disabled also needed to dwell within an organization big enough to cooperate with other entities while maintaining its own unique identity. I sought out organizations with which to partner, such as Campus Crusade, the Christian Medical and Dental Association, and InterVarsity Christian Fellowship. I also investigated World Medical Missions/Samaritan's Purse and YWAM. Though some seemed like a fit in many ways, we couldn't forge a partnership with any of these.

So the work continued as a semi-independent, supplemental service of Kijabe Hospital. Rehab operations there had increased from 113 in 1989 to over 400 in 1992. Polio, clubfoot, and cerebral palsy were the most frequently encountered disabilities. Christoffel-Blinden Mission (CBM) provided funding for two new rehab operating rooms with some other added facilities. International Rehabilitation Mission,

Inc. purchased a new Land Rover for the mobile clinic work. Funding for surgeries came from CBM, the Liliane Fonds, and churches and individuals; they seemed to recognize the value and potential of our work with the disabled, possibly even before I did.

In 1995, the Kenyan government gave approval for Kijabe Hospital to train interns. Up to this time, interns had never been trained outside of government hospitals. One of the first of these was Dr. Joseph Theuri[52]. In October 1997, after completing his internship, he joined me to be the first rehab trainee. He was an excellent doctor. We added one new rehab trainee each year. After three years, Dr. Theuri went to Uganda for formal orthopedic training. Following that training and some further time with me, he became the first national orthopedist and medical director for our facility, Bethany Crippled Children's Centre, which will be described in Chapter 8.

By 1996, we began making regular trips to Kakuma Refugee Camp, near the northern border of Kenya. The team was usually composed of a high school graduate who helped organize our mobile clinics, a brace maker, and me. The majority of the refugees were Sudanese, but there were smatterings of Congolese, Rwandans, Burundians, Ugandans, Ethiopians, and Somalis tucked into this remote, dirty, hot camp. There were about 85,000 people there at that time. We saw women with vesicovaginal fistulas, but primarily we saw disabled children. None of the countries from which these refugees fled had well-functioning medical programs. Whatever programs they did have became worse in the midst of civil conflicts. This was especially true for the disabled.

Our usual routine at Kakuma was to see patients on three

52 See profile in Appendix.

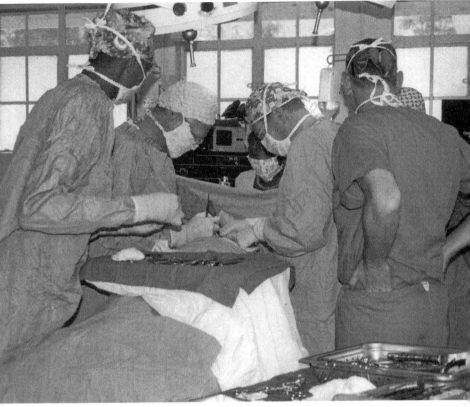

Dick and Dr. Ben Warf in the BCCC operating room

mornings and teach selected refugees about disabilities in the afternoon. The refugees we trained became community-based rehabilitation workers and were scattered throughout the camp. The education level of these workers varied greatly – from only a few years of primary school to a few years of college. Their language skills also varied significantly.

The refugee camps, first at Kakuma and later at Dadaab, not far from the Somali border, opened up a vast source of neglected, disabled children. BCCC became nearly the only facility available to care for the needs of the disabled for these camps. While we did most of the pre- and postoperative care at the camps, it was a nightmare trying to coordinate the transfer of patients from the camps to Kijabe.

My Elijahs continued to arrive in Kijabe. Dr. Louis and Anne Carter began working and teaching at the hospital in 1996. Anne, an operating room nurse, improved the skills of many of our operating room technicians. Louis brought with him not only tremendously needed skills in hand and plastic surgery, but also a very evident compassionate heart. They usually came for one to three months at a time. Their visits were eagerly anticipated, and children from all over Kenya made the trip to Kijabe to see them. The Carters also traveled to Kajiado, Joytown, and other locations to evaluate patients.

Louis cared for patients with deformities from burns, snakebites, congenital hand deformities, cleft lips and palates, and many other abnormalities. I learned 99% of what I know about burn contractures and plastic surgery from him. One unique thing about Dr. Carter was that he never wanted to operate alone. He recognized each operation as a teaching opportunity and wanted other doctors to be in the OR to learn from him.

Louis was a surgeon who saw beyond the operation and recognized the need for occupational therapy to maximize the function of the hands on which he operated. He not only took time with our physical therapist but also arranged for a special hand therapist to visit Kijabe and share her skills with our resident staff. A few patients returned intermittently for years allowing Dr. Carter to fine tune the results.

He also brought instruments and materials that could not be purchased by most mission hospitals on limited budgets. He left many instruments and books at Kijabe. For years his library remained in our home between visits and it was a precious teaching tool even in his absence.

Our mobile clinics were going well. Before too many years had passed, we were traveling to 15 clinic sites where we provided pre- and postoperative care. These trips sometimes provided me with learning opportunities of a different sort. I called them my "Flight School Lessons."

At the end of one of the trips to Kakuma, we hastened to the rocky runway and loaded our luggage into our small plane. We were making an extra stop in Korr and wanted to leave as quickly as possible in order to get back to Nairobi that afternoon. Jeff Barnett, our pilot (one of Dr. Bill's great-nephews – there are Barnetts all over Africa) reached into his pocket for the key. However, the key was not there. Not a problem because usually there was a spare under the cowling. He removed the cowling. No key. We all joined the search and checked every nook and cranny under that cowling. No key.

Meanwhile our driver went to the camp to check Jeff's room, looking for the key. Nope, still no key.

Jeff radioed Nairobi to confirm the normal location of the spare key. Unfortunately, we had already looked there. So it was time for Plan B. Jeff and his counterpart on the other end of the radio went over the details of hot-wiring an airplane.

To me, hot-wiring was what car thieves did on the streets of North America. And now my pilot — no petty thief, of course! — was going to do this to the airplane in which I was going to be flying.

First, we needed a long piece of wire. To my surprise that was cut out of the guts of the airplane, sacrificing a light on the tail. Then Jeff leaned down into the engine and attached

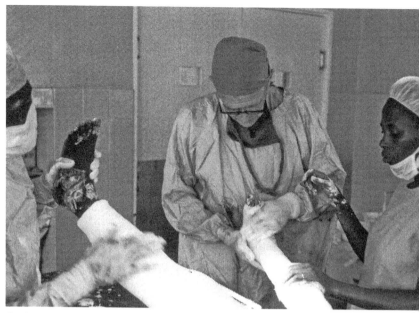

Dick in Kijabe Hospital operating room, approximately 1996.

the wire to something. He then passed the other end of the wire up and threaded it through the right window, next to where I was to sit. Jeff's head disappeared beneath the dashboard of the plane to pull up another wire.

We boarded and my job was to press the ends of the two wires together, creating the circuit to start the engine. Voila! The engine roared to life. I separated the wires, and I cannot remember any other details. The plane took off. We were on our way to Korr, a small frontier town in northwestern Kenya.

I first visited Korr in 1972. It is the home of the Rendille, a very colorful and, until recently, Unreached People Group (UPG), a term that always made my heart beat faster. The term refers to a group of people who have not yet heard the Gospel of Jesus Christ. My first contact with the Rendille had been in 1966 when I was a medical student. At that time, there were very few, if any, Christian Rendille.

It was fun to be there again. I removed the casts of a few children who had had clubfoot operations. We put on their braces. I visited a young lady, Intaynoy, who had had polio. I had operated on her a few years previously. She was now walking rather than crawling.

This side trip was very fulfilling. As we were leaving, one of the missionaries, Lynn Swanipoel, walked me to the plane. She and her husband had spent years translating the Scriptures into Rendille and had seen very little spiritual fruit. But recently they had begun holding literacy classes at the nursery school. She told me that they now had a "problem." There were so many Rendille coming to the Lord that they were not able to adequately disciple all of them. I thought that this was a wonderful problem! God had done a wonderful work among the people in this tribe. But it had taken perseverance for over 40 years.

When we were all settled on board, I dutifully pressed the "hot wires" together and the engine sputtered to life again. We flew over Ngurunit, Mt. Kenya, Naivasha, the Ngong Hills and soon landed safely back in Nairobi. I had mastered Flight School Lesson 1: Hot-wiring. But even more amazing was the wonderful work that God was doing in the lives of the Rendille.

"Flight School Lesson 2" occurred on another memorable safari (trip) to Kakuma, also located in the northwestern corner of Kenya. It was a very hot afternoon when we boarded to leave. The team included Daniel, Peter, Steve, and me. Daniel organized our clinics; Peter was an orthopedic technologist; Steve was the pilot. Peter had flown for the very first time only two days previously, and he was excited. So we all agreed that he could sit in the co-pilot's seat. I sat behind him, and Daniel was to my left, behind the pilot.

Our pilot, Steve, gave us instructions about the exits on the Cessna 206, the emergency supplies in the rear, and the safety belts. He explained about the turbulence that often occurred during afternoon flights and the airsickness we might experience. He pointed to the black plastic bags and informed each of us about their use.

Flight check. "Clear prop!" And we were climbing into the sky. The air cooled off and I was about to settle in for a much-needed nap. But about twenty minutes into the flight Steve turned to me asking if I had any antacids. I gave him some. Shortly afterward, Steve vomited all over himself and the instrument panel. Then he passed out!

I had made more flights than the others on the plane, so, by default, I became the commanding officer. I turned to Peter and told him to hold the steering wheel. In a matter of seconds many thoughts came to mind. I was subconsciously sure Steve was dead. If he were dead, I wondered how I would pull him back over the front seat and crawl into the pilot's seat. I wondered if I could get the radio working well enough to find someone who could "talk me down." Undoubtedly, I prayed too. All of this occurred in a few very short seconds.

Suddenly, I remembered that before we left Kakuma I had grabbed a bottle of frozen water from the refrigerator and stuffed it into my bag. So I pulled out that icy cold, partially frozen bottle of water, opened it, and dumped the whole thing over Steve. To everyone's surprise and relief, he woke up!

Flight School Lesson 2: Always carry an ice-cold bottle of water with you on a flight into the bush.

Steve radioed AIM-Air in Nairobi seeking advice. He pulled out maps trying to identify a landing strip. Simultaneously, each of us began searching the ground for an airstrip. We were flying over northern Kenya, which is desolate and very, very sparsely populated. We located a landing strip and Steve buzzed it before making a perfect landing. The four of us crawled out of a rather smelly airplane.

Steve, lacking clean clothes, changed into one of my less-polluted shirts and pair of trousers. I cleaned up the interior of the airplane. Steve weighed the decision about what would be best. Should another pilot be flown in to ferry us back to Nairobi? He spoke to the leadership in Nairobi and they decided to allow him to continue the flight.

This time I was the one who crawled into the co-pilot seat. Steve repeated the flight check and the instructions to each of the passengers. I watched more carefully this time, still realizing that it would be a miracle for me to land a plane even with someone "talking me down." Fortunately, our trip to Nairobi was without incident. When we arrived, many of the AIM-Air staff were waiting outside the hangar to welcome us.

We never knew why Steve became ill. Some thought that he might have had food poisoning. He returned to flying a few months later and, as far as I know, nothing like that has happened to him since. But it certainly was a flight to remember!

After that, life took on new meaning for me. Millie and the kids assumed a higher level of importance, and I was a more thankful fellow. I also did a lot of personal soul searching. If the objectives of caring for the disabled were to include travel, fatigue, and danger, would it be worth continuing? Yes! We would not hesitate to push on.

The chapter began with Nehemiah 5:16: "I persevered in the work on this wall, and we acquired no land, and all my servants were gathered there for the work." Nehemiah rallied his people to complete the reconstruction of the wall around Jerusalem. This was seemingly an impossible task. What I desired to build, with the Lord's guidance and blessing, was a ministry that could meet the physical and spiritual needs of disabled children from all over Kenya, and maybe, eventually, all of Africa. Many building blocks were falling into place. The mobile clinics were up and running and poised for expansion. Funding streams were being identified. New surgical options were being added to our repertoire. Most importantly, a growing group of dedicated staff members, both administrative and medical, began finding their way to Kijabe. We still had acquired no land, but the servants were certainly gathering for the work.

CHAPTER 7

Exploring New Territory (1996)

"The steadfast love of the LORD never ceases; his mercies never come to an end; they are new every morning; great is your faithfulness." Lamentations 3: 22, 23

One Sunday in 1995, a Samaritan's Purse tour group came to our home for lunch, followed by a visit to our pediatric ward, and a time of sharing about the work with disabled children. Two pastors from Calvary Chapel, Gary Kusunoki and Ed Cornwell, were among the group. In April 1996, those two pastors returned to Kenya and called one afternoon asking if they could visit the following day. Most who came to visit were interested in the work with the disabled, so I asked, "Would you like to see the hospital?" They simply replied, "No," but did not enlighten me further about why they were coming.

For the next 24 hours I pondered the purpose of their visit. The following afternoon they arrived. Millie served tea and, after the normal small talk, they told us about their plans. They were going to visit the Nuba Mountains in Sudan the next day and then return in July with a team. Sudan was a powder keg, embroiled in a civil war since 1983. Few charter airlines were willing to fly into Southern Sudan, and even less willing to fly into the Nuba Mountains. According to the Sudanese government, all unapproved flights, including "mercy flights," were illegal. No one knew what the consequences might be if that edict was violated. Most just chose not to consider them.

RICHARD BRANSFORD

I asked politely, "Is there any way that I can help?" They said, much to my surprise, "Yes! Would you join the team as our medical doctor?"

I was already busy developing the work with disabled children and my other hospital responsibilities. In addition, I was a happily married man who wanted to continue my marriage, so I turned to Millie for permission. I don't believe Millie ever forbade me from embarking on such ventures, even when they involved some danger. She was sensitive to the Lord and content with nearly all of my decisions. In 1992, she agreed to my participation in a relief effort to Somalia for three months with Samaritan's Purse. In 1994, I helped Samaritan's Purse in Rwanda during the genocide.

Now I was asking her once more. Would she agree to me flying once again into a war zone? She nodded her approval.

A few months later, their team arrived in Nairobi. It was made up of pastors and non-medical workers. Teaching, preaching, redeeming slaves, and showing the "JESUS" film[53] were their main objectives. The slaves were mostly children, with some women. Slavery was real, and this was the twentieth century.

As spiritual as the plans sounded, many other logistics needed to be resolved. Just getting there would not be easy. The team needed to plan for food, purchasing medications, preservation of the anticipated vaccines, means of electronic and verbal communication, camping items, and innumerable other items.

Some of us were actually excited about the meals. Ed, who had been a chef in a rather fancy restaurant before

---

53 http://www.jesusfilm.org

122

becoming a pastor, was to gather the food items for the team. Unfortunately, there was no need for excitement. The meals consisted of chocolate Power Bars for breakfast and lunch, and repeated doses of canned beef stew for supper. Oh, well...it was sad to see such culinary talent go untapped.

More medical personnel were needed to complete the team. My daughter Bethany, now a graduate nurse, was in Kenya for the summer. She volunteered to help locate and purchase medication and prepare medically for the trip. They invited her to accompany us and she agreed. Now they had a doctor and nurse on the team.

Although Bethany had previously been in Rwanda, I was concerned about her coming with us into Sudan's war zone. I had never worried very much about putting myself at risk, but this was significantly different.

The evening before we were to depart, the team realized that Bethany was the only female on the team. They asked me about bringing our other daughter Susie, who had recently finished her first year at Asbury College where she was studying English. She was excited about the opportunity. My anxiety increased another notch.

Two planes were hired. Because the previously planned site, the Nuba Mountains, had recently endured major military battles, a new site was decided upon: Nyamlel in Bahr el Ghazal. I flew in the first plane with Walt Shepard, Bill Agius, and the governor of the region. We were to land a few hours before the rest of the team was to arrive. Our group was expected to scout out the area and decide where to set up camp.

As we flew across the huge open African plain, I spoke with the governor. He was a lawyer and a former SPLA (Sudan

People's Liberation Army) fighter. Nyamlel was his home. Making "doctor" small talk, I asked, "What happens to ladies in labor who need C-sections?" He casually commented, "They just die. The nearest facility that could do a C-section is 300 miles away." That was beyond my imagination. In retrospect, I suspect death was so common there that almost nothing was shocking to those who lived under those conditions.

We landed, unloaded the plane, and it left. We brought water and tents, but very few other items in this "advance" plane. No food, communication equipment, sleeping bags, or other items that one might normally consider essential, especially in an isolated area of a country at war. But we were not concerned because the other plane was due to arrive in only two hours.

We explored the area and saw evidence of previous battles. Buildings from yesteryear, intended to be permanent and enduring, had been reduced to crumbling and neglected walls. The hospital that had been envisioned decades before remained a mere foundation, covered with weeds and small trees. A mud and thatch structure served as the only medical facility.

We meandered through the market and found only okra and Sudanese tea available from the few functioning shops. This was by no means a traditional, abundant African market like those in Kenya. I saw no cows in the area, possibly only a few goats. Land was plentiful, but we were told that very little of it was cultivated.

A few stray horses wandered around. We asked about them. We were told that northern armies had periodically come down by train and swept across the land on horseback, killing, stealing, and enslaving women and children. The few horses left behind belonged to riders who had not survived the raids.

The local Dinka people were constantly fearful, plagued by persistent and traumatic memories of those violent raids. Starvation inevitably followed the war and we saw gaunt adults and children throughout the village. We three normal-sized adults appeared very well nourished in contrast to our hosts. And of course, our very white skin contrasted shockingly beside their very black skin. They openly stared at us as we walked among them.

We set up our camp at the old clinic previously run by GOAL[54] and waited for the second plane. Two hours passed. Three hours. Four hours. It was getting dark. Many thoughts ran through my mind. The uppermost was that this was a war zone and flights, like ours, were officially illegal. Where were my daughters?

The governor, recognizing our peculiar situation, invited the three of us to have dinner at his house. Thanks to the darkness, we could not see exactly what we were eating. That was likely fortunate. The meal included okra, but that was all we could identify. Walt, who had been raised in Congo, commented later that he had eaten a lot of different things, but this was the worst. We were grateful to have something to eat, and we survived.

It was a long night. The tent helped keep out the mosquitoes, and we slept (or tried to sleep) in our clothes using our backpacks for pillows. Our concern about the second plane kept some of us tossing and turning. As soon as there was a faint hint of light, we began surveying the sky and wondering.

About ten o'clock, an Antonov plane roared onto the landing strip and quickly lowered its loading ramp. Materials and people, including my two very-much-alive daughters, came tumbling out. The plane never shut down its engines and was

54 https://www.goalglobal.org/

off as soon as everyone and everything was unloaded. I was later told that if the pilot shut down the engines he would have had to wait at least 45 minutes until they cooled down in order to take off again. The pilot did not feel it was safe to have the plane sitting on the ground that long. Therefore he kept the engines running. I stood beside that strip and silently expressed my thankfulness to God. My daughters were safe and we were together.

Crowds had already gathered at the clinic. Some of our team headed there, carrying medical items. Others carried supplies to the campsite.

In the midst of all of the busy-ness of that day my daughters explained what had happened. They had flown from Nairobi to Lokichoggio, near the Kenyan border with Sudan, on a plane that I believe was called a G3. It was refueled at Loki and then took off headed toward Nyamlel.

That was when the "strangeness" happened. The pilot heard a message on his radio telling him to "turn back." He knew, of course, that all flights not approved by the Khartoum government were illegal. So he returned to Loki, landed, and went to the control tower. At the control tower, he asked about the message he had received. The controller told him that he knew of no such message. It had not come from him, and he had no idea where it originated.

The confused pilot walked back toward his plane. On the way, a friend, who was also a pilot, asked him where he was headed that day. He told him, "Nyamlel." His friend asked him what he was flying. He said, "A G3." His friend replied, "You will never make it in on that strip!" Apparently a G3 could not land on the small airstrip at Nyamlel. An alternate airplane, an Antonov, was located. The G3 was unpacked and everything was transferred to the new plane. However, it was too late to fly that day, and the team remained in Loki overnight. There was no way to inform us what had happened because we had no suitable communication equipment at Nyamlel.

Who sent that message? We never knew, but we had suspicions (another angel?) and we were thankful.

> *If I take the wings of the morning*
> *and dwell in the uttermost parts of the sea,*
> *even there your hand shall lead me,*
> *and your right hand shall hold me.*
> Psalms 139: 9,10

The clinic ran well that day; we were busy. We chose to make immunizations our first priority, feeling that ultimately they would save the most lives. They included DPT (Diphtheria-Pertussis-Tetanus), measles, polio, and BCG (Bacillus Calmette-Guerin).[55] I taught Susie how to mix vaccines and helped her give her first injections. Those were gigantic steps for a first-year English major!

It became evident as the day wore on that it would be better to break into smaller teams the next day and go to three sites rather than have all of the patients come to Nyamlel. A place just beyond the river beside Nyamlel seemed appropriate for a second site and would allow more people to access the care. A third site 10-12 miles away was more of a challenge, but this was situated in a large village. Each remote site would require its team to carry cold boxes, supplies for immunization, and some medicine.

I would remain at the clinic in Nyamlel to treat routine medical illnesses such as malaria and worms, as well as a myri-

---

55 BCG increases resistance to tuberculosis.

ad of other disorders that would undoubtedly demand significant guesswork to treat. I presumed that there were only three of us with sufficient experience in Africa to lead the medical teams: Bethany, Susie, and me. We chose Susie, with less than 24 hours of experience, to be the team leader at Site 2 across the river. She would be closer to camp in case she needed help.

Site 3 obviously had to go to Bethany and her team. It was a long walk and included some wading through swampland. But Bethany was willing. We had our usual Power Bar for lunch and beef stew that night. I could only imagine some of the thoughts swirling in the minds of the members of the team. We were a diverse group, ranging from older people, probably in their sixties, to high school twin boys with vivid imaginations and lots of energy. Each team leader tried to determine what was reasonable and safe, considering that we were in a very isolated area in a country that had had the longest civil war on the continent. Each team would travel with a line-of-sight radio, which was the only communication device we had other than a satellite phone. Each team included a more experienced member for logistics. They would each have a GPS with alternate sites already identified as potential gathering points in case of emergencies.

That evening we gathered together for devotions, prayer, and planning. Everyone was excited — and a bit anxious. Below us, about 50 yards away, was the river. We could hear the echoes of thousands of night insects. We could also hear the melodic sounds from the village drums nearby, singing, and the occasional piercing screams of women. Later, we were told that these screams were just a part of the singing of this culture. However, I wondered if there might be a connection to some pagan practices.

The next morning, Susie's team crossed the river to Site 2 with supplies and some untrained members of the local Dinka tribe to help. She was also covered with lot of fatherly prayer. She spent the day immunizing children, and it was a busy, but satisfying, day for her. (Many years later, she said this trip was one of the reasons she changed her career plans from English to nursing.)

Bethany and her team left early to cross the river by canoe and trek many miles to get to the more remote Site 3. In some places the swamp water came up to their thighs. They were always concerned about the threat of marauding crocodiles, leeches, and other creatures. None of these predators attacked our team, thanks to the multitude of people praying.

They arrived at Site 3 after about three hours. A crowd of people seeking medical care and a large number of children needing immunizations mobbed them as soon as they appeared. Little medical care had been available in this village for possibly 20 years or more. Unfortunately, the throng became so unruly that the clinic work had to be prematurely terminated.

In the midst of this chaos, Bethany met an emaciated, elderly grandmother holding a terribly malnourished baby girl named Adut. Adut was about 10 months old and weighed approximately 8 pounds. A translator told Bethany that the baby's mother had died. The grandmother had been keeping her alive by feeding her milk obtained from other mothers and from goats. After much deliberation, Bethany suggested to the grandmother that the team take Adut back to Nyamlel where we could rehydrate her, feed her, and give her medications, with the understanding that the grandmother and father would come to Nyamlel the following day to retrieve her. They agreed.

Bethany and her team began the long trek back to Nyamlel. Bethany sang to little Adut during the miles of hiking, shook her occasionally to assure herself that she was still alive, and thought of names that she might call her. Adut just didn't seem like a pretty name to this American nurse. Bethany wanted a new name, one different from those that she had cared for in Rwanda in 1994, those who had died. Those names carried special memories for her. "Great is Thy Faithfulness" was one of the songs she sang over and over again during the hike, so she settled upon the name Faith. Faith Adut.

Susie's team had been back at camp for quite some time. Again I was an anxious father. Bethany's team didn't arrive until well after dark. They had been forced to use some of the emergency light sticks included in each backpack to find their way the last few miles. I met Faith and we soon developed a care plan - rehydration, calories, antibiotics, and a lot of prayer and love. We used 4 x 4 gauze as diapers and sandwich bags with the corners cut out as plastic pants, although they were actually big on her. In a labor of love, Gary, Susie, Bethany, and I each took turns walking, holding, and caring for Faith throughout the long night.

I was walking Faith in the wee hours of the morning when Eddie, one of our team members, came to me with a big insect attached to his leg. By "big" I mean huge! It was Eddie's first trip to Africa and, to his credit, he stayed calm as he asked me if I knew what this strange creature might be. Was it a leech? No. But I didn't know what it was. Together we bid a hasty goodbye to his uninvited guest.

In the morning, Faith appeared somewhat better. The day was busy with clinic, the care of Faith, and the visit of Faith's father and grandmother. I felt that Faith could probably only survive if she were taken out of Sudan and given professional medical care over a longer period of time. But taking her out would mean that she would probably never return to Nyamlel, and this would involve even more far-reaching plans. This was explained to the father and grandmother, and they seemed to understand. With their fingerprints, they thoughtfully "signed" a letter composed by the governor-lawyer-SPLA fighter giving us custody of the little girl.

The vigil for Faith continued through another night. Gary, our team leader, felt that because Bethany had brought Faith to camp, the Bransford family should have the prerogative of adopting Faith. We had adopted Joshua a few years previously, and I honestly thought that Millie felt that we were a bit too old for any future adoptions. So I told him that we would decline. Gary used the SAT phone to call his wife, Carol, in the U.S., and she agreed to welcome Faith into their family.

The following day was another clinic day and a day caring for Faith. That evening, the "JESUS" film, in the Dinka language, was shown to a very large crowd, and many, if not all, expressed their desire to become Christians. The response was so surprising that we were not certain how to interpret it. We doubted that many, if any, in that remote location had ever heard a true presentation of the Gospel. We were certain that they had never seen any presentation like the "JESUS" film. There was no electricity within probably 150 to 250 miles. There were no schools, reasonable roads, medical facilities, or any of what we westerners thought of as "modern amenities" for living. And there were certainly no Starbucks.

Day 5 was the day for part of our team to speak more specifically with pastors and new Christians. Even some of the pastors made a new profession of faith. It was a day of rejoicing and also a day of preparation. Some of the local Dinkas were taught how to use the film projector, which we were leaving behind, along with the "JESUS" film, generator, and extra fuel. To the best of our knowledge, the film was later taken all over the countryside. I am absolutely certain that many came to the Lord through the showing of that film.

Later, the Northern Army brought troops into the area and captured the film, generator, and projector. This was used as obvious evidence (to them) that western powers were helping the SPLA.

Early the following morning, we were up, packed, and ready to return to Kenya. With everything on board the two planes,

Bethany, Faith, Dick, and Susie

a picture of Bethany, Susie, Faith, and me was taken. It's one of my favorite pictures. We had fewer supplies going back, but we had one extra, special, little person.

It was Sunday morning and our plane flew low over the Nile valley. On and on we went for probably an hour and a half. Thatched huts stood perched on stilts over the Nile. Birds, the only wildlife we saw, flew lazily between the earth and us. As we got further south we passed over Bor, a large town in Southern Sudan, and saw a huge thatched church in the shape of a cross. We had lots of questions, but no answers, about this church.

After about four hours, we landed in Lokichoggio and moved into a larger plane that could accommodate our whole team. The airline was rather a cowboy outfit, and there were not sufficient seats or safety belts, but at this phase of our adventure, that didn't really bother us. A young African woman who ran a camp in Lokichoggio approached us. She asked if she could hitch a ride to Nairobi. We had plenty of room and wanted to help, so we welcomed her aboard.

We chose to delay our official entry into Kenya until we arrived in Nairobi. We still didn't know exactly how we would get Faith through immigration. We only had a few handwritten pieces of paper to authorize our custody of her, signed by the unrecognized governor of Bahr el Ghazal in an unrecognized country. During the flight, our African guest approached Bethany. She recognized and understood our dilemma and kindly asked what we were going to do with Faith when we arrived in Nairobi. Bethany and I told her that we didn't know. She responded, "Just give me that baby, and I will carry her through!"

And that's exactly what happened. Our newfound friend,

dark and beautiful and known to the immigration officials, breezed through immigration with Faith, equally dark and equally beautiful, securely in her arms. The authorities didn't even take a second look. Could she have been another of God's angels?

We arrived in the early evening without diapers, formula, bottles or any of the normal accoutrements of new parents, so we quickly drove to the home of a young couple I knew and begged for help. They were only too happy to assist us, and we went to our hotel with everything we needed.

Faith stayed in the Bransford home in Kijabe, doubling her weight in two and a half months. After about five weeks, Carol Kusunoki arrived from the U.S. and joined us. Two weeks later, Gary and their two daughters arrived and they took Faith to their apartment and began to oversee her care. The Kusunokis, after many frustrating months of effort, were finally able to adopt her and have raised her as their own. Faith recently graduated from high school and lives in Southern California with her adoptive parents and sisters.

It would appear that we Bransfords had missed the opportunity to invite Faith into our family, but maybe the word "missed" is wrong. It somehow implies failure. I would like to think that our on-the-spot decision not to adopt Faith was God-ordained and eventually led to an alternate plan that was more perfect in His eyes. Did the Master Designer have something else in mind? We were about to find out.

CHAPTER 8

Following God's Directions (1996 – 2009)

"But when Jesus saw it, he was indignant and said to them, 'Let the children come to me; do not hinder them, for to such belongs the kingdom of God. Truly, I say to you, whoever does not receive the kingdom of God like a child shall not enter it.' And he took them in his arms and blessed them, laying his hands on them."
Mark 10: 14-16

In July 1996, just prior to going to Sudan, Bethany visited New Life Home for Abandoned Babies[56] in Nairobi. The founder told her about Philip. He had been born on October 13, 1995 at Kenyatta National Hospital. His mother was ill and apparently felt it best to abandon him one day after his birth. He was taken to New Life Home. A few weeks later Philip developed salmonella meningitis (a very rare form of meningitis caused by salmonella bacteria) and subsequently hydrocephalus. He had a shunt inserted at Aga Khan Hospital. He was still there when Bethany visited the home; they only had a photo of him to show her. They felt that he was not a good candidate for adoption because of the possible complications associated with his shunt and the potential expense of his future medical care. Bethany said, "That wouldn't be a problem for my parents. My dad puts in shunts!" The staff immediately began praying that we would adopt Philip.

------

56 http://www.newlifehometrust.org/

Their prayers continued for four months. Although Bethany had briefly mentioned her encounter with Philip, during much of this time we were busy caring for Faith. But in November, before flying to Lamu on a surgical trip, I had an extra hour before the flight. So I made an abrupt, unplanned visit to New Life Home. I knocked at the door and introduced myself to the staff member who answered. She commented, "We have been praying for you!" I saw Philip that day and recognized that his development was delayed. I could not stop thinking about him during my trip to Lamu.

Upon my return, I nonchalantly mentioned to Millie that there was a little boy at New Life who needed a home. She didn't seem to catch the hint. However, on December 10, she drove Chris, Beka (Chris' wife-to-be) and Saca (a friend and RVA dorm parent) to the airport for their trip to Israel where they were to join Susie and Jon who had been studying there. As she and Joshua were returning to Kijabe, Millie felt a very strong urge to turn off the main road and visit New Life Home. While (almost) 4-year old Josh played with the babies, she watched Philip. One of the workers was tickling him and his delighted giggling was charming. But she would not hold him. There was so much to consider.

On the way home, she told Josh, "There was a baby there named Philip who needs a home, but we must know what God wants – if we are to take him or not. God showed us clearly that you were to be a Bransford and if that is true for Philip, He will show us. Let's pray that God will give us a definite sign, okay?" So they prayed in the car as they drove home.

Later that day, I sat at the kitchen table clearing out my 1996 appointment book and transferring various papers into the new 1997 one while Millie prepared supper. I came upon a poem that Bethany had sent us and said to Millie, "Look at this!" She began to read "Pray for the Children" by Ina Hughes:

We pray for children

Who put chocolate fingers everywhere

Who like to be tickled...[57]

By that third line, Millie burst into tears and cried, "We must go get Philip! God wants us to!" She was sure the poem was the definite sign from Him that she and Joshua had requested in prayer. At the same time, she remembers thinking how dumb it seemed, humanly speaking, and how dumb others would think we were taking another small child at our age, 56 and 53!

On December 17, 1996, we brought Philip home. On Christmas Eve, Millie, Josh, Philip and I drove to Nairobi where we spent the night at Samaritan's Purse awaiting the arrival of Chris, Beka, Saca, Jon and Susie. We were to pick them up at the airport at approximately 3 AM. However, the plane arrived early, so they caught a taxi to Samaritan's Purse and surprised us. But, we gave them an even greater surprise - a new baby brother! Up to that moment, they had known nothing about Philip.

With Philip, our family was complete (or at least I think it is). Although we didn't have 14 girls and three boys like we had envisioned in 1964, our two daughters and five sons definitely filled our lives and our "quiver[58]"!

On the professional front, surgical and rehabilitative

57 See Appendix for full text.
58 Psalm 127: 4, 5

services for the disabled continued at Kijabe Hospital. Scott Harrison, orthopedist and entrepreneur, first arrived in early 1996 to provide short-term orthopedic coverage and to look at our work with disabled children. Scott was a very experienced orthopedist, but also had administrative skills. He had helped an orthopedic equipment company recover after a financial downturn. He seemed to like what he saw in our relatively young work with the disabled at Kijabe. I explained to him that I had not felt it best to place the expanded development of this work under the Africa Inland Church (AIC), but he encouraged me to continue to explore the church's possible involvement.

I visited Bishop Birech, an older, godly pastor, who was then the Bishop of the AIC. He was warm and friendly, and seemingly optimistic about our work with the disabled. He suggested that I investigate an expansion at Kijabe by utilizing the facility where a once thriving, but now languishing, radio studio was located. This was directly across from Kijabe Hospital.

While the potential of the location seemed intriguing, this soon became a frustrating experience. All of the land and facilities of Kijabe Mission Station were owned by the AIC, and there was no way we could obtain true ownership. "Remuneration" became the key word in our negotiations. Rather than purchasing the land and facility, we remunerated the radio committee for their assets. With those funds, the committee could construct a more suitable facility on land already offered to it elsewhere at Kijabe. It took a lot of time and turmoil to settle on a figure, but we eventually reached an agreement.

Organizations and people interested in the expansion of

the work with disabled children offered their assistance. We pushed ahead with the development and plans were drawn up. In 1997, we broke ground.

A new organization, Bethany Crippled Children's Foundation (BCCF), was registered in the U.S. in 1997. Millie and I chose "Bethany" because it was the place where Jesus rested[59] and it was a biblical word that would not offend non-Christians. We liked that. Plus, it's our daughter's name, and she has a huge heart for children. In June 1998, we held the dedication for the 30-bed Bethany Crippled Children's Centre (BCCC). It was to provide elective orthopedic and reconstructive surgery for disabled children.

However, although those coming for care prior to 1998 had been primarily those with orthopedic disabilities, burn contractures, and cleft lips/palates, the number of children coming to us with hydrocephalus was beginning to increase and I wanted to help them too. In 1999, I read an article about the International Federation for Spina Bifida and Hydrocephalus (IF).[60] IF had recently begun working in Tanzania. At the bottom of the article was an e-mail address. I wrote to the address to ask if they knew where I might purchase inexpensive (I am embarrassed to say that I probably said "cheap") shunts. Then I waited for a reply. And I waited. And waited.

I didn't realize that the main office for IF was in Geneva. Mr. Pierre Mertens, the president of the organization, lived in Belgium and only reviewed e-mails periodically. Finally, Pierre wrote back and asked for more details about our work. That seemed peculiar to me, but I told him about the increasing number of children coming to Kijabe with hydrocephalus. I also shared that I was a general surgeon and inserted shunts

59 Matthew 21:17
60 http://www.ifglobal.org/en/

only because there weren't enough doctors inserting them in Kenya, at least not at an affordable cost.

Pierre wrote back suggesting that they would "just give us the shunts that we needed!" Hallelujah! Thus began a longstanding, wonderful relationship with IF that continues to this day. In 2010 IF provided us with at least 500 shunts, plus other shunt-related materials, the salaries for some nurses, and help with transportation costs for 15 mobile clinics scattered around Kenya. It also helped establish the House of Hope, a guesthouse in Kijabe to accommodate the families with disabled children who come for care at the hospital.

Dr. Jim Wade (who first came to Kijabe to do cleft lips in 1995) continued to bring a wonderful menagerie of people, including other ENT and plastic surgeons, family practitioners, nurses, anesthesiologists, and others, to Kijabe once or twice a year. Among them was Mary Jordan, who was employed by Glaxo Wellcome, a pharmaceutical firm. She was not a pharmacist, but, while at Kijabe, oversaw the distribution of the donated medicine that accompanied this team.

Mary was inquisitive. She asked many questions about BCCC, my work, how the work had begun, growth, etc. She undoubtedly asked similar questions of other staff at BCCC, and even others outside of the hospital.

After returning to the U.S., Mary received a fellowship to the Brookings Institute in Washington, DC. As part of her fellowship, she worked in a Senator's office and investigated the national government's role in medicine. She began e-mailing me with inquiries about my need of a 501(c)(3) entity, separate from that of Bethany Crippled Children's Foundation (BCCF), to help in the care of the disabled.

Honestly I initially did not want to even consider this. I

rationalized that BCCF was created to function in that role. I had directed my friends and other donors to contribute through BCCF. I wanted to believe that relationship would be long-term. But Mary recognized that even good organizational relationships could experience friction as their missions grew, sometimes in different directions. The more I considered Mary's suggestion to create a separate charitable entity, the more I recognized her wisdom.

I knew nothing about the information needed to apply for a 501(c)(3) status, but Mary recommended a lawyer, Matt Downs, who was willing to do the work *pro bono*. He patiently guided me through the time-consuming process. Finally, all was in place, and we filed a formal application with the U.S. government to establish Bethany Relief and Rehabilitation International (BRRI). I take full responsibility for this rather bulky name. I thought it would identify BRRI's objectives. We have participated in both rehabilitation and relief work. But, as others pointed out, our emphasis is on rehabilitation services.

Plans were made for the first board meeting to be held in Washington, DC, in the Senate Office Building on Monday, September 17, 2001. I invited Dr. Ivan Stewart, Dr. Jim Wade, Miss Mary Jordan, General Scott Gration, and Miss Patti Mechael to serve as board members. I was to fly to Canada to speak at a pediatric surgery conference, and then proceed to Washington for the board meeting.

On the afternoon of September 11, Bethany called from Nairobi with the news about the Twin Towers disaster. Millie went up to RVA where satellite TV was available. Later Joshua, Philip and I joined her in the TV room where the footage of the airplanes crashing into the towers was shown over and over again. We were overwhelmed.

The Jomo Kenyatta International Airport immediately closed but soon reopened with new, rigorous baggage inspections. On Wednesday afternoon, the day after 9/11, I flew to London, but there were no connecting flights to either the U.S. or Canada. The following day I was able to fly to Toronto and travel by bus to Kingston where Dr. Ivan Stewart lived. We were still uncertain if our Sunday flight to Baltimore would take place. Fortunately, it did.

We arrived at the Gration home and discovered Scott had been in the Pentagon when the plane crashed into it. Thankfully, he was unhurt. That evening, Judy Gration took us to the Pentagon to see the damage. The scene was full of people speaking in hushed tones, lighting candles and setting up impromptu memorials.

On September 17, Matt Downs attended BRRI's first board meeting to explain the official documents, which we discussed throughout the day. In the evening, we continued the meeting at the home of the Grations. Finally, BRRI was officially birthed. We had no idea what the future might hold.

From 1998 to 2004, our hospital work with the disabled was confined to the 30 beds available at the BCCC facility. An increasing number of children began to arrive with hypospadias[61], imperforate anus[62], Hirschsprungs disease[63], hydrocephalus, spina bifida, cleft lips/palates, and many other problems. Many were not elective cases. Treating them would require a change from the original approach of BCCC, which was established primarily as a facility for elective orthopedic

61 An abnormality of the urethra in which it ends on the undersurface of the penis.
62 A congenital abnormality in which the anus is not present at all, or the opening is in an abnormal position. Often there is an abnormal connection into the vagina, urethral, or to an abnormal location on the perineum.
63 An anatomical abnormality of portions of the colon with abnormal, usually decreased neurological function.

rehab. To further complicate the matter, the 30 beds available at BCCC were not even sufficient to meet those existing orthopedic needs. The BCCC board decided that unless sufficient funds could be put in reserve to meet the medical expenses for an anticipated increase in the number and variety of new cases, the size of the facility could not be increased.

In January 2004, a majority of the Board at the BCCC facility decided that children with hydrocephalus and spina bifida should be moved back to Kijabe Hospital. This would alleviate the overcrowding at the facility. The 36-bed pediatric ward at Kijabe Hospital had been underutilized with only an average of 12 to 14 beds typically occupied. With some renovation and adaptations, it would be sufficient to house the hydrocephalus and spina bifida patients.

BCCF changed its name to CURE and assumed full management of the former BCCC facility. It continued to serve primarily children with orthopedic needs. Bethany Relief and Rehabilitation International (BRRI), in association with Kijabe Hospital, assumed care for children with hydrocephalus and spina bifida.

This separation was difficult for me. BCCC was a dream that had evolved over many years. The friendships and relationships that I had developed with staff and patients at that facility were very important to me. The disruption in those relationships was deeply stressful and, in an odd way, felt almost like a divorce.

But it became clear as time went on that Scott Harrison and I had different visions. I must quickly add that this in no way implies that the ambitions or methods of either of us were necessarily wrong. They were just different. Scott wanted to develop a wider, international network of hospitals primarily for the orthopedically disabled. This is, indeed, the path that CURE International has taken since 2004. In fact, the facility at Kijabe was the first of many CURE hospitals scattered around the globe.

In contrast, my vision was focused on expanding the work to serve a wider variety of disabilities within Kenya and East Africa. So our organization moved in that direction. After months of composing a Memorandum of Understanding with the Kijabe Hospital, the new entity, called BethanyKids at Kijabe Hospital (BKKH), was given sufficient liberty to oversee the hospital's entire children's ward and one operating room. This seemed adequate to meet the needs of children with hydrocephalus and spina bifida for the foreseeable future. The agreement also included the freedom to establish a small outpatient facility for disabled children adjacent to the ward, oversee the day-to-day quality of nursing care, select our staff, and give additional training to our nurses.

But there were many details in this agreement that definitely reflected a compromise by both parties. Kijabe Hospital was a large institution with a multitude of significant interests. The work with disabled children was, and is, only a relatively small part of the hospital's overall mission. Some of us involved in this work were concerned that services to the disabled, without a champion to secure their place at the table, could quickly lose support and significance within the larger hospital environment. Oscar Ogwang, hired to oversee the renovations at the facility and the transition to the hospital, aptly described the partnership between the hospital and BethanyKids (BK) as being like a "marriage between an old person and a young person." He stayed with BK and managed that dynamic for nine years, seeing us completely through the transition.

On November 1, 2004, all the children with hydrocephalus and spina bifida at the CURE facility were physically moved across the street into the newly refurbished BethanyKids at Kijabe Hospital (BKKH). Agnes Jeruto[64], a nurse administrator at BK, described the scene as being like "Moses crossing the Red Sea" with the Israelites – children in front, workers carrying luggage and equipment behind them.

Astonishingly, all 36 beds designated for BKKH were full at the end of the day. By April 2005, BKKH was given an additional eighteen beds. Eventually, we had a total of 67 beds available for disabled children at BKKH. Even then, we sometimes had to put overflow patients in the halls. In February 2006, BRRI, which was overseeing the work and was less than five years old, began contemplating expansion.

Again, we looked at establishing an independent 120 to 200 bed children's hospital. It was hard to forget the failed negotiations for the Grant Estate in 1992-1993, but some of us still longed for an independent facility focused on the care of disabled children. We were still looking for a true dwelling, a home of our own. In 2007, another property, located about 25 minutes from Kijabe, was identified as a possible site. "The Ranch" contained between 240 and 250 acres and had magnificent water sources. Also, two potential electrical supplies were nearby. It seemed like an ideal location for a rehabilitation facility.

BRRI entered into a Memorandum of Understanding with the property owner; funds were raised toward its purchase. We needed $500,000 by a certain date; thankfully, we had this in hand. However, by 2008, it appeared that the sale would not go through. It was another deep disappointment to me. In one

---

64 See profile in Appendix.

of my prayer letters in 2009 I wrote, "My only conclusion was that God, in all His wisdom, knew what was best for us and this work."

In the end, BRRI decided that it would be more effective – medically, educationally, and spiritually – to continue working with Kijabe Hospital. Many obstacles stood in the way, but somehow many of these were resolved.

Behind the dark clouds that characterized this period of time are shining silver linings. After the separation, BKKH and CURE together had nearly 100 beds available for disabled children, as well as other sick children. BethanyKids staffing and range of services expanded. Many of the pediatric nurses received additional training in the care of pediatric patients and disabled children. Now, BKKH cares for not only children with hydrocephalus and spina bifida, but also for children with other congenital anomalies. Training programs in orthopedics, including orthopedic rehab, as well as pediatric surgery and pediatric neurosurgery were established. General surgery residents with the Pan African Association of Christian Surgeons[65] (PAACS) began coming to BK for three months of special training in pediatric surgery. By 2010, 3000-3500 operations were being done each year on disabled children. In 2010, 716 shunts procedures were done. The number of spina bifida closures had increased from 8 in 1997 to 301 in 2010.

The stories of some of these special young patients are included between this chapter and the next. They are the true heart of the ministry and reason for its existence. If I had had my way and restricted the work with the disabled to the 30-bed Bethany Crippled Children's Centre alone, much less would have been done for them and fewer would have been

---

65 http://paacs.net/

served. Oh, how narrow our vision, my vision, so often is! Thank God He overruled my limited human perspective!

GLADYS TALLAM

Gladys was born in July 1991, in the Baringo District of Kenya. Medical staff at the hospital immediately recognized that she had spina bifida and referred her to Kijabe Hospital. I closed her back when she was four months old and her parents

Gladys Tallam

diligently took her for follow-up to the mobile clinic in Nakuru where they learned how to better manage her condition.

When Gladys was six years old, the BCCC staff taught her mother how to do clean intermittent catheterization (CIC). She faithfully did that every six hours until Gladys was a teenager. Then she was taught how to do it herself.

But she deliberately neglected CIC, fearful that other students at school would see her and misunderstand. She threw away the catheters given to her by the mobile clinic team. Instead, she took folic acid with the mistaken idea that it would treat her incontinence. Eventually this backfired. Her kidneys became infected, and she developed a pressure sore that needed surgical care. But she put off the operation on the pressure sore for two years.

About that time BCCC workers contacted her and asked if she would participate in a conference on spina bifida. She reluctantly agreed. There she met other SB patients in wheelchairs and realized that she was one of the few who could walk. Francesca Maina[66] was there and pointedly asked her if she was doing CIC. She admitted that she wasn't. One day she followed Francesca into the bathroom. She secretively looked through a small hole in the wall as Francesca catheterized herself while using crutches. Gladys was amazed that Francesca could do it so easily even while on crutches! She decided then and there to do CIC regularly.

At first her bladder was holding less than 20 milliliters of urine. She was introduced to oxybutinin, a medication that enabled her bladder to hold urine for a longer period of time. Eventually she was able to extend the intervals between catheterizations from 2 to 6 hours. She was then scheduled for the

---

66 See Chapter 9.

skin graft for her pressure sore, and it finally healed after nine months.

After finishing high school she received some computer training and further instruction about spina bifida and hydrocephalus by the BK team at Joytown. She then began the process of following up older children who had had spina bifida closures as infants. We wanted to know their outcomes and complications. She also worked with teens at BK, teaching them about CIC and foot care.

Now she has completed her nursing training at Kijabe College of Health Sciences. She has a special heart for teenagers and youth with SB because of the special challenges they face when they are that age. She's turned her disability into an opportunity and confidently asserts, "God gave me this challenge for a reason!"

PHILLIP M.

It was December of 1996 when I first met Phillip's father. It was a Saturday when I received a call from the Outpatient Department of Kijabe Hospital asking me to come. Rather reluctantly I went down to find a father holding photos of his 8-month old son. The father had come a long way, nearly 300 miles, just to see if we could help.

As I gazed at the pictures of his son, I realized that I had never seen this combination of deformities that included all four extremities and also the face and forehead. (Later I learned that this was officially called "amniotic band disruption complex/sequence.") His legs had multiple deep grooves and his hands had some digits missing and others were deformed. But he also had a bilateral cleft lip and palate and a large defect in the nose and frontal skull.

When thinking surgically, our first consideration is often, "What can't I do?" But also, along with that thought, emerges another: "What can I do?" Both thoughts came to me, but the dominating conclusion was, "What can we do?" I could do some repairs on the deep grooves of the legs. The ENT team coming in the summer could handle the cleft lip and palate. Dr. Carter, a plastic surgeon expected later in the year, could also help.

As the story unfolded, I learned that an Operation Smile team had already seen Phillip. They felt that he had so many significant deformities that they didn't believe that it was wise for them to begin his care during their brief visits to Kenya. They suggested that he come to the U.S. where he could receive better care by a diversified team of specialists. His parents waited several months but never received any further communication from Operation Smile.

Thus began our long relationship with this young family. In January 1997, nine-month-old Phillip arrived for the first stage of a multi-stage repair and underwent Z-plasties[67] to both legs, thereby removing the deep grooves that ran around his legs and hopefully improving the circulation. In June 1997, Philip had his bilateral cleft lip repaired. Unfortunately part of this broke down, likely due to his very exaggerated prolabia, the central soft-tissue segment of the upper lip. In October of that year, after treating Phillip for an ear infection and malaria, Dr. Carter did a "vomer recession with premaxilla setback[68] along with a repeated repair of the lip." This repair provided a

67 A technique in orthopedic and cosmetic surgery in which one or more Z-shaped incisions are made, the diagonals forming one straight line, and the two triangular sections so formed are drawn across the diagonal before being stitched.
68 In lay language this means that the middle part of the front of his hard palate was moved back to allow the lip to close without too much tension.

remarkable improvement in young Phillip's appearance.

Maybe our white coats encouraged Phillip to be a bit grouchy. Maybe he just associated us with needles, operations, and pain. Maybe he just had been through more surgeries than most people experience in a lifetime. Whatever was the cause, Phillip often did not welcome us to his bedside.

His kind mother, a teacher, was very thankful for what had been done for her little boy. She talked graciously and prayed with us. This little boy was God's gift to her. Why the deformities? Why the expense? Why the pain? Why the great disruption of their home? We can't answer these questions, but God knows. Perhaps this was a means to soften hard hearts. Perhaps this was a pathway to lead the parents and Phillip to the Savior. Perhaps He just wanted to teach all of us something. God knows, as He knows in the case of all of the children that come to us.

"The field is white unto harvest" and includes people like Phillip. He is remarkably better, and we can praise God for that. It was worth the trip down to the hospital on that Saturday morning. Jesus' command "to go into all the world and preach the Gospel" includes the world of the disabled. The "harvest is great, but the laborers are few." Thank you God for Phillip!

ANTHONY

It was July 24, 1996. We will probably never know the whole story of that day.

Anthony was 7 years old when his home in Thika caught fire. His mother, a widow with five young children, was in a nearby building and unaware of the fire. When the fire began Anthony rushed outside carrying his sister Catherine. The two suffered minimal burns. He then realized that his three-year-old sister Mary remained in the house. He re-entered the burning house and rescued her from certain death.

Anthony was taken to a local hospital with major burns. He received only minimal care for three months. When he was finally brought to Kijabe, I saw contractures, open granulating flesh, and even bare bone. The scarring had left his face distorted. The left side of his face was drastically burned. His left ear did not exist; there was just a hole where it once had been. Thus began the "Saga of Anthony."

We debrided (cleaned up) and dressed his face, scalp, arms and hands. Over the next few days, the base of the wounds became cleaner. There was a deep infection over the left side of his skull. Dr. Louis Carter, a visiting plastic and hand surgeon, recognized that Anthony could not close his left eye. This often will lead not only to a dry eye, but also an infected eye and possibly scarring and blindness. Dr. Carter released the contracture of his left eyelid and placed a full thickness skin graft, allowing his eye to close. Later the left side of the skull was grafted also.

Although he was a disagreeable (some might say stubborn) little guy during dressing changes, his overall joy remained despite the burns that had marked him. He could often be found walking around the hospital grounds holding a balloon. He laughed when tickled and enjoyed singing Gospel songs. His favorite one was about Jonah. Earlier in his life when only four or five years old he had heard the message of salvation at Sunday school and had come to know the Lord as his Savior.

The teaching of "laying down his life for his friends" was more than just words to this little lad. He returned to the hospital for several more operations, and when he came, I always introduced him as "my hero." I really meant that. He will have scars for the rest of his life, but they are truly "red badges of courage."

FAZIRA

I had been to Bukaleba, Uganda before. A traditional witch doctor lived there. Not far from this little village there was a large rock where daily animal and food sacrifices were offered to the "spirits." Life was a struggle here. The Basoga people were desperately poor and barely eked out a living. I suspected that the death rate was high and few had much hope.

In 1997, my friend, Web Carroll, a long-term missionary with Global Outreach, asked me to see a little twelve-year old girl. Her name was Fazira and she crawled on all fours. We entered her small, crude, thatched-roof hut where she lay on a grass mat as I examined her. She had contractures of her hips and knees and very little muscle activity in her legs due to having polio when she was very small. She was an ambitious student in spite of her disability and had crawled a mile each way to and from school every day for several years.

I told her young mother that a few relatively simple operations could be done, braces applied, and that her daughter should be able to walk with crutches. However, she would have to bring Fazira across the Uganda border to Kijabe for surgery, an eight or nine-hour drive.

Web had thought that nothing could be done for her and he was very excited about this possibility. Three weeks later he brought Fazira and her mother to Kijabe Hospital. Operations were performed and a spica cast[69] applied. Her legs

---

69 See previous footnote on Sala's profile.

and waist were essentially immobile, but straight. She was to remain in the cast for a month. When the cast was removed, she would wear braces on both legs. The hard part would be learning to walk.

This mother and child could not communicate with staff while at BCCC because Basoga is an unknown language at Kijabe. So Web brought a young Basoga man to visit them. He also brought their much-beloved traditional food and the "bread of life," the Gospel. Impressed by the loving care at the hospital and the message of the Gospel, Fazira's mother left the Muslim faith and committed her life to Jesus Christ.

About a week after the operation Fazira returned to Bukaleba, still in the cast. Crude wooden parallel bars were built outside her home in preparation for teaching her to walk. One month later, the cast was to be removed. There was no cast cutter, so Web and his wife took Fazira and her mother to their home, put Fazira in a bathtub of water and "left her to soak" for a few hours. Slowly, and with difficulty, the cast was peeled away. A Ugandan physical therapist helped her mother put on Fazira's braces, and she soon took her first hard steps.

As Fazira took those physical steps, Fazira's mother took her first spiritual steps. She was the head of the local health committee, so she called a meeting and publicly confessed her newfound faith in Christ. Soon afterward Web saw Fazira's polygamist Muslim father waving down his car as he drove along the road. Hesitantly he stopped, for he assumed that he was angry. However, the father asked him the way to eternal life, and he too became a Christian.

About a year later I visited Bukaleba and asked about Fazira. I was directed to her school. She literally came running toward me on her crutches, now needing only one brace for her leg. She seemed so happy.

A door opened through this little girl's disability that allowed the presentation of the Gospel to her family and community. Similar doors are opening throughout Kenya and other parts of Africa. Medical centers for the disabled are needed throughout the developing world. The task is bigger than we are, but we pray the Lord will give us not only vision, but also the means to meet this challenge.

JANE NJOKI KIMANI

Jane is a petite, outgoing young woman with sparkling eyes and a bright smile. She fearlessly drives her little car through the unbelievably congested and chaotic streets of Nairobi. It is hard to imagine that she ever had a disability that required surgery.

When Jane was born it was very obvious to her community that she had a problem. The people of her village called her "the disabled girl," and that offended her and her family. Her care was mismanaged at several hospitals and eventually someone "whispered" to her father that he should take her to Kijabe.

Her parents enrolled her at Joytown in Thika, and through BCCC's mobile clinic Jane was one of the kids brought back to Kijabe for treatment. Jane had had several operative procedures done on both feet before I first met her. Both feet were small and their growth had been severely compromised. Our hope was to make her feet more functional. Each foot had procedures done to attempt to straighten them, and there was significant improvement. However, she was destined to have very small feet.

She loved her years at school in Joytown where disability is the norm. "Joytown, for me, is a wonderful place. I played and played and played. I didn't realize I had a disability until I left!" After finishing her primary education at Joytown, she went on to enroll in Mary Hill School, one of the best secondary schools in Kenya. Her siblings understood and Jane got "first priority" in education.

One afternoon in 2006 I received a call from our rehab outpatient department asking me to visit with a young lady who knew me. When I arrived at the hospital I saw Jane. I had not seen her in a few years, and, in fact, I am not sure if I had seen her since she was a primary student at Joytown. She was now a young lady, but I recognized her.

She told me that she had just graduated from the University of Nairobi with a bachelor's degree in Education, Accounting and Economics. She had come to say thank you for what I had done to help her. I was overwhelmed with the extra effort she had taken just to say thank you. We talked for a while and, as she prepared to leave, I told her that if she were ever looking for a position, she should consider BethanyKids. Sometime later she called and submitted an application. Soon Jane joined us at Kijabe.

Jane worked with me at BK from 2006 – 2011. She wrote grant proposals, headed the implementation of mobile clinics, and worked in the administration. She also managed special projects at Joytown, talking to teachers and other workers at the school to determine what the needs were. Many of those workers still had pleasant memories of when Jane was a student there.

At that time, a donor had offered funding to help with a project at Joytown. Covering the walkway was considered to be the most pressing need. The path was full of ruts and puddles and was very difficult for children to negotiate with wheelchairs and crutches.

Jane presented the proposal to me and I asked her to oversee the project. This included repairing the walkways and putting a roof over it to keep it dry. She was to locate contractors, request bids, and award the contract. This was the first project she ever formally implemented on her own. She was fearful because it involved money, and she thought, "What if I make a mistake?" But she remembers being told, "Even if you lose money, you will have learned something." She needn't have feared. The project was a success.

For about a year Jane was one of the ladies from BK who attended Millie's weekly Bible study in the evenings. The ladies would gather early for dinner in our home, and they would fill one large table. Josh, Philip, and I, and any other male visitors, dined at another table on the porch. Then we men would "disappear," allowing Millie and the ladies the use of the living room. I would usually retreat upstairs to the computer where I could occasionally hear bursts of laughter. It was a real joy to have these young ladies in our home.

In 2011 Jane chose to leave BethanyKids and return to Nairobi. In 2012 she received her MA in Project Management. She also is a Certified Public Accountant. Her most recent position involves conducting baseline studies and supporting the implementation of IT-enabled services in Kenya for an International Trade Center.

Jane accepts her problem without feeling "disabled." She makes the most of life, choses joy over sadness, and brings happiness into the lives of many others.

She hasn't had any operations since high school, and her

feet have grown stronger with time. She wore braces and special shoes for many years, but now she leads a normal life. In college, "I got to campus and wanted to look nice. Now I wear all sorts of regular shoes, as long as they're comfortable!" she says, and adds with a laugh, "And also nice-looking!"

SOPHY

You usually knew how Sophy felt. Her usual response to a greeting was a broad smile that melted your heart. She frequently arrived with a lollipop. We teased her about her lollipops. Sometimes I brought her a lollipop, but more often she brought me one. Her lollipops were some of my most precious possessions.

Sophy was born with spina bifida at Nakuru Provincial Hospital on December 14, 1998. Within a short period of time five other children with the same condition were born at that same hospital. The nurses told all the mothers that their children would die within two months and consequently the other five mothers decided not to care for their children.

Jane spent the night in prayer. She prayed that God would either let Sophy die that very night, or she would take her home to care for her. In the morning, Sophy was still alive. She took her home and told her family, "Sophy will die when God wants her to. Not when anyone else wants her to, because I know God has a purpose for Sophy." Her own mother thought she had gone mad, but she stood her ground.

Shortly thereafter, when she was less than a month old, Sophy was brought to Bethany Crippled Children's Centre. Not only did she have spina bifida, but she also had hydrocephalus. Her back was closed and she had a shunt inserted to lower the

Dick, Sophy, and Jane (Sophy's mother)

increased pressure in her brain. Jane recalls that the BK staff was so caring and supportive. They would hold Sophy when she cried. Jane was so relieved. Finally she was able to sleep through an entire night.

We saw Sophy a few times each year. She had many complications, including shunt malfunctions, pressure sores, bladder infections, bouts of pneumonia, and a strange coma that recurred eleven times during her short life. Sophy never walked and she struggled with school. But her smile and her encouraging demeanor was a great encouragement to me.

Jane is one of the bravest women you'll ever meet and was totally devoted to her daughter. She carried Sophy on her back to and from school every day, even when she was a "big girl." She faithfully did her CIC, fed and bathed her, and made sure she was comfortable. In September 2015, I learned that Sophy was ill. In early October God decided to take her home. I will miss her smiles and her special lollipops.

MERCY MUTHUMBI NG'ANG'A

Chaplain, BKKH

Working with the disabled is more than just about healing bodies. It's about healing souls as well. Chaplain Mercy Ng'ang'a organized our spiritual program in 2005. The Lord uniquely prepared her for this important ministry.

As a young woman, she attended Moffat Bible College in Kijabe and then trained as a laboratory technician at Kijabe Hospital. Following her training, she went to Lokori, a remote, frontier mission station in the Northern Frontier District. The Turkana people there live a traditional, nomadic life. (Some would even call it primitive.) Mercy worked in the laboratory at the Lokori Mission Hospital while sharing the Gospel with the Turkana.

There she met her husband-to-be, Joshua, a schoolteacher in a government school in Lokori. After they were married, they became involved in a variety of ministries. Joshua was extremely talented in many areas, and he had a lot of common sense. Joshua and Mercy both taught at the AIC Missionary Training College in Eldoret, and eventually Joshua became the hospital director for AIC Githumu Hospital.

They had five children and were doing well until 1997 when Joshua developed aplastic anemia[70]. He spent a year going back and forth to Kijabe for blood transfusions. He became a

---

70 A disease in which the bone marrow and the blood stem cells are damaged, causing a deficiency of all three blood cell types.

candidate for a bone marrow transplant at a hospital in South Africa. However, while they searched for a donor, Joshua developed an overwhelming infection. In his final hours Mercy read Scripture verses to him about heaven and he told her he was "going home." He passed away three days before his scheduled departure for transplant surgery.

It was a hard time for Mercy. Funds were tight and she was left with five children, three in secondary school and two in primary school, to raise by herself. But she prayed for guidance and God told her, "Mercy, I'll never leave you, nor forsake you. I'll help you with your children, all the days of your life."

She went to live with her widowed mother for a year, built herself and her children a small house out of corrugated metal, gardened, and allowed the Lord to heal her heart and ease her grief. One day in 1998, Dr. Tim Fader, a family practitioner from Kijabe Hospital, stopped to see her. He told her that Bethany Crippled Children's Centre was about to open and asked if she would consider coming back to Kijabe to be the X-ray and lab tech.

She was reluctant at first, but finally came for an interview. She was offered the position as a lab and X-ray technician. Mercy faithfully performed this role from 1999 to 2005 and felt God leading her to interact more with the mothers of the children. But she fought with God for about a year while continuing in her role as a lab technician at BCCC.

In 2004 Bethany Kids at Kijabe Hospital began its work across the street from Bethany Crippled Children's Centre (CURE). In 2005 Mercy applied for the position of chaplain. At that time she said, "I knew people would talk back to me, and I don't like people talking back to me!" she laughs. She also didn't consider herself a "people person." But she became

Mercy Ng'ang'a, conducting Bible study on the ward

BK's chaplain and, she said, "I never looked back."

Mercy goes from bed to bed each day and sits with the mothers and children, telling them about Jesus. She is able to empathize with nearly every problem they have, because she's experienced many of them herself – poverty, lack of a father in the home to help with the children, lack of resources. Using this gentle, "come-alongside" approach, she normally sees over 600 people come to the Lord each year on the pediatric ward.

Rehab patients usually are seen over a long period of time, so it is an ideal situation for sharing the Gospel and discipling people. So Mercy initiated the "Disciplers Program," a highly effective way of spreading the message of Jesus and ministry to the disabled throughout Kenya. She trains Christian women who have been associated in one way or another with BKKH how to:

- Visit and encourage new believers who are returning to their home areas,

- Share the Gospel in a village context, and

- Assist patients in practical ways to keep their follow-up appointments at local mobile clinics.

To date over 500 disciplers have been trained. Between 2005 and 2014 over 37,000 people have come to the Lord through this ministry. Praise God! I used to smile at Mercy and say "10,000"! She knew what I meant. Now I have to say the "next 10,000!"[71]

When a young patient dies, Mercy is nearly always there, day or night. She comforts tearful mothers, prays with them, and gives them hope of the same "home in heaven," that God gave her after her beloved husband's death so many years ago. She says, "All the glory goes to God! He lifted me up for His own reasons."

---

71 Often, with much encouragement, Mercy would get me a list of those saved during the year by November. I would write a Christmas letter. At the bottom I would write the names, 5 in red and 5 in green - over 1000 names. One friend told me that he would print it out sand drape it across his living room.

CHAPTER 9

Remembering Special Ones

"For you formed my inward parts; you knitted me together in my mother's womb. I praise you, for I am fearfully and wonderfully made. Wonderful are your works; my soul knows it very well." Psalms 139:13

The vision of helping the disabled might be compared to a sunrise on a particularly dark night. All is black, and then the light barely peeks over the hill giving a faint blush to the valley. Each minute, more is exposed and details become clearer. Likewise, the needs of the disabled have become more apparent with time. People with diverse skills have joined together to provide for them. Financing this effort has never been easy. Some of our "wants" have not yet been fulfilled. But God has, in His wisdom, sufficiently provided.

I recognize my work with the disabled was truly a learning experience. Even the venture into training disciplers grew from a longing that was built on prayer. We were so green. But God came down! I am not talking about the little "g" god, but about the big "G" God of the entire universe. He came down and dwelt among us, blessing us in ways that we could have never imagined. No, that is not to say that we did not have our complications and disappointments, including patient deaths, but He seemed to pour forth an extra portion of Himself upon us and upon those who, in desperation, came to us. For many years I didn't realize that disabled children and their outcomes were the real reason that I began to feel truly fulfilled.

Jesus said, "Let the little children come to me and do not hinder them, for to such belongs the kingdom of heaven."[72] What profound words these were to me! Jesus, Savior, would take time from His busy schedule to invite the children to come to him. Couldn't I do that? Didn't I need to do that? Didn't I need to get my priorities straight? Weren't these little, disabled kids a major part of why He had put me on Earth?

God often cautioned me to keep my eyes on Him and not on difficult circumstances that pressed in more often than I liked. He would take me out into our ward, filled with children – my "little ones" – with hydrocephalus and spina bifida, and remind me that they were the reason He had brought me so far. He brought Daisy into my life and I think that He spoke encouragement and peace into my life through her. When she awoke from the operation and could move her left arm and leg…well, that really spoke into my life.

The death of little patients was never easy. I have seen a lot of children die and have been with a lot of young mothers who feel that God has abandoned them. Because I treated children with hydrocephalus and spina bifida, I realized patient deaths would be more frequent. In the midst of this, I purposefully reminded myself of the patients who did well, who came through the battles, in spite of the cost. While I had my valleys, I also had my mountaintops. I thank God that He walked through them all with me.

In the years of change and the periods of exhaustion, reflecting on the following two patients revived my passion as a child of God to press on in the effort to improve surgical options and services to children in the developing world.

------

72 Matthew 19:14

MICHAEL

It was 2000, and the Bethany Crippled Children's Centre team was doing a Friday clinic in Nakuru. We were in an old run-down building adjacent to the War Memorial Hospital. On a typical day we would see 100-150 children with a wide variety of disabilities. Some of the patients were follow-up cases and some were completely new. On that day I escaped from the confinement of the tiny examining room to the porch. The benches out there had been pushed end-to-end for possibly 30-40 feet; they were full of patients. So I sat at one end and had them slide down the bench to see me and be examined.

One young lady finally had her turn. Her son's face was covered, but this was not unusual in Kenya. She told me that he was just a few weeks old and had been born with a problem. She then removed his blanket. My heart skipped a beat as I stared intently at this little boy, named Michael. He had a very large nasal encephalocele, which is a defect in the skull that allows dura, cerebrospinal fluid, and some brain tissue to escape from the normal confines of the skull. Other changes made this little boy even more unique. His right eye was concealed behind the large, cystic mass and some pigmented nodules extended up the right side of his forehead.

I wondered what to tell this young mother. His condition was somewhat urgent, and its "remedy" far beyond my skills. There were areas in the cystic mass covered with thin tissue, raising the possibility that it might rupture. I explained to her that a neurosurgeon would be necessary to repair this defect, and I was not a real neurosurgeon. One would be coming to Kijabe within a few months. She seemed satisfied, though concerned, and I arranged a future appointment.

A few weeks later, while I was away from Kijabe, I received

a telephone call telling me that "Mama Michael" had come to the hospital. Michael's mass had ruptured and fluid was escaping through the open wound. I knew immediately who this Michael was. It was Friday and I was not scheduled to return until Sunday. I did not know what to do. There were no other doctors at Kijabe better prepared to care for this child, and I recognized that my skills were insufficient. I ordered sterile dressings to be applied and started him on antibiotics.

During the rest of the weekend, Michael was continually on my mind. Upon my return on Sunday I immediately went to see him. The large protuberant mass on his forehead was gone, leaving a collapsed piece of abnormal skin in its place. My first instinct was to take him to the operating room the next day, debride this (clean it up), and dress the wound. Mark Newton[73], a pediatric anesthesiologist, and I discussed the case and decided to try to close the defect from the front. This would be a much longer operation than initially planned, and a major infection could be expected.

On Monday, Michael was put to sleep for his operation. I raised the loose tissue to find a bone defect one centimeter in diameter extending into skull through an opening beneath the orbit. In order to secure a real closure, this defect had to have vascularized tissue[74], be "water-tight," and be able to resist some pressure. I considered this a nearly impossible expectation, given my limited surgical skills and experience with this type of defect. We cleaned the area over and over again, and then, I raised some periosteum[75] from over the maxillary sinus and tried to fold it in. Periosteum normally promotes new

73 See profile in Appendix.
74 Tissue that contains vessels that carry fluids in the body.
75 The connective tissue that envelopes the bones other than the articular, or joint, surfaces.

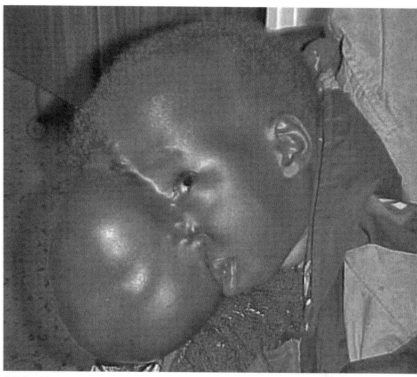

Michael

bone growth, and it can be a fairly strong tissue. With this raised, I sutured it together in the center over the defect. I did not think that this alone was sufficient; we would need other soft tissue around this to provide strength and added blood supply. But, skeptically, I patched these thin layers over the defect. I was worried. Finally, we took the best skin remaining from the defect and closed it, attaching it to the tissue beneath it. Michael, humanly speaking, was not beautiful at this time, but his wound was closed. Now, would it heal? Could it tolerate the inevitable infection that might destroy our repair? I kept him on antibiotics, and fortunately he never demonstrated any overt evidence of infection. A CT scan done later suggested that his brain was reasonably normal.

I eventually learned that Michael's mother was very, very

poor and I strongly suspected that she sold herself to provide for her infant son. During their visits to Kijabe, and later Nakuru, I felt privileged to hold little Michael in my arms and pray for him. I also would give some money to his mother to help her. She was very needy. This too was a privilege. I grew to really love this young mother and her child.

Toward the end of 2002, Michael, now nearly 2 years old, was admitted again. The pigmented lesions extending up over his forehead were deforming. Dr. Louis Carter was planning to come, and we had decided that an operation could be done to remove the lesions. However, as a first stage to this repair, Michael would need a tissue expander to stretch the skin. This is like a balloon with saline inside. The volume of saline is slowly increased to gently stretch the skin. His blood count was adequate and an expander was inserted.

Following this procedure, Michael ran a fever that antibiotics did not resolve. I had a sudden, upsetting thought. I combed his old charts, looking for his HIV test results. I was so certain that I had previously done an HIV test. When I couldn't find them, we tested him. Michael and his mother were both positive. My heart was very, very heavy.

We removed the tissue expander and his fever finally abated. We could not put him and his mother on antiretrovirals (ARV)[76]. This was relatively early in the hospital's ARV treatment program. The policy was to treat only those patients living within a 20-mile radius of Kijabe so the hospital staff could provide supportive care and be relatively certain the drug regimen was continued. Because Michael and his mother lived beyond this radius, they were not candidates for ARV treatment at Kijabe. We did refer them to a center in Nakuru,

---

76 Often referring to materials/drugs that are effective against retroviruses. Retroviruses inject a copy of their DNA genome into host cells in order to replicate.

but treatment was never begun.

They returned home and made regular visits to see us at the clinic in Nakuru. We did what we could and prayed for them. A few months later, Mama Michael died. Michael's uncle and his family took over his care for the following months until Michael also died. Once again, my Father had taken one of my little waifs and welcomed him into His family.

I began writing this chapter about Michael in December in the mountains of North Carolina. This morning I went for a walk. It was cool, but not really cold. The skies above were mostly clear with the slightest fingernail moon. A progressive blush of sunlight touched the eastern sky. The hues became richer, then, just as suddenly, began to fade. Deer peeked at me from an open field. I rounded a curve in the road to see the valley below shrouded in puffy, mashed-potato-like – or perhaps cotton-candy-like – fog.

I imagined God up in Heaven with Michael and his mother sitting beside Him. All things had been made perfect. You could almost touch the love that poured between them. All things had become new. I imagined one day I would come into their presence and know Michael and his mom, not by their external appearance but by something else more enduring. What is that something? I do not really know. I would like to assume that we will just know each other, profoundly and deeply. I look forward to that day. Until then, we live, as C.S. Lewis put it, in the "shadowlands."

FRANCESCA

Francesca Najipu Maina is a living legend among many of the disabled in Kenya[77]. She has touched so many lives, it

77 You can watch Francesca's testimony at https://www.youtube.com/watch?v=8pKrOYXJ1KY

is hard to fully assess the impact she's had. It's all the more amazing, considering when she was born her grandmother wanted to kill her.

Peter, Francesca, and Jeremy

Francesca was the second-born of eight children. Her family was from the Samburu tribe with a culture very similar to the Maasai. She was born with spina bifida. She couldn't walk well, couldn't feel her legs, and was partially incontinent. Her father called her a "useless child," wouldn't talk to her or include her in any family activities. Her mother did her best, but their family life was difficult. Although Francesca felt discarded and unloved, she persevered.

Eventually she walked slowly to and from the neighborhood school every day, a walk that took two hours one way. If class started at 8, she started walking at 6. Sometimes there would be an elephant in the way! She would just wait until the elephant passed by and then continue her walk.

She developed pressure sores in her legs, but couldn't feel them. Sometimes she'd have a stone in her foot, but she didn't feel that either. Sometimes her leg would swell with infection and she would miss school for days at a time. She began wearing "gumboots" (rain boots) even when it was very hot, because they prevented stones from becoming embedded in her feet. She was constantly wet with urine; the other children avoided her. She took sweets to school to give as bribes, seeking in any way possible to have friends, even if it was only for a few minutes.

By the time she was 12 years old she was seriously depressed. She tried to commit suicide twice and wondered why God didn't just let her die. She stopped going to school and spent her days sitting outside her house, doing nothing.

One day a pastor, new to the village Pentecostal church, stopped to see her. He asked her why she wasn't at school and asked about her family. He asked if she was lonely and if she had anything to do. He brought her a small radio and encouraged her to listen to some music. Francesca agreed. He came back again and asked if he could pray for her. She agreed. Then he asked her if she wanted to come to church. She explained that she couldn't walk alone, but he said he would walk with her. So he came and they walked slowly to church. He introduced her to the congregation and asked them to welcome her. His wife and children walked with her, even when she was wet. It amazed her that they didn't care about that. They just wanted to love her.

"I loved that pastor so much. I always listened to him. I

asked him to teach me about Jesus. He told me that even if nobody else loved me, Jesus did." So she gave her life to Christ.

Soon thereafter, her Uncle Simon, her father's younger brother, also gave his life to Christ and enrolled in Moffatt Bible College in Kijabe. People there told him about the hospital, and he told them about Francesca. He asked his brother, Francesca's father, if she could come there. Her father agreed, but refused to provide any funds for her transportation. So money was raised through the Samburu community, and Francesca finally went to Kijabe. It was 1997 and she was almost 19 years old.

She recalled that she had "never seen so many wazungu (white people)!" She was told there was a doctor who should see her, but he was at a mobile clinic. That was Monday. They told her to come back on Thursday. She did and they sent her to the operating room waiting area.

I came out of the operating theater and saw her sitting there. I looked at her leg, which had a very infected pressure sore, and then asked to look at her back. I told her uncle that the problem was her back, that she had spina bifida, and the nerve damage was affecting her legs and bladder. (It was not an open SB, so it wasn't apparent to non-medical people.) For the first time in her life Francesca knew what was actually wrong with her.

We put a cast on her leg, hoping to promote healing. The cast was on for two weeks. When she returned to the hospital, the leg was still not good. Reluctantly, we realized that we would need to amputate her leg. Neither she nor her Uncle Simon had money for the operation. We told them that many crippled people came to see Jesus and He never turned them away. We would not turn her away.

We explained everything to her. We also told her about God. She wondered if I was a pastor or a doctor. Many missionaries in Kijabe visited her and shared the Word of God with her. The first verse she memorized was Jeremiah 29:11: "For I know the plans I have for you, declares the LORD, plans for welfare and not for evil, to give you a future and a hope." She wondered about that — God had a plan for her, a poor, disabled Samburu from the bush?

After the amputation, she was deeply worried, "I feared that I would never be able to walk again." However, she was fitted with a prosthetic leg and taught to walk with crutches. The bill for her care was huge. She didn't know how it was paid; she was simply told that it was "clear." She was one of the first SB patients to be taught clean intermittent catheterization (CIC). That procedure changed her life. She was no longer constantly wet, and she no longer smelled like urine. "My life changed day by day," she said. "I started to have hope."

BCCC offered her a job. Although she didn't have any education, two missionary women taught her how to give Sunday school lessons to the children. An African pastor helped her finish a three-part course on how to teach the Bible lessons. Once she successfully completed her course work, Francesca was hired as Children's Mentor.

Being among the first employees at BCCC, Francesca helped at the hospital when equipment and supplies arrived. She later worked in the playroom and on the wards. She shared her story with the young patients, telling them about the love of Jesus. Many children and their parents came to the Lord. She accompanied us to mobile clinics where she would talk to mothers about how they could better help their children. Francesca said her life was transformed "medically, spiritually, and socially."

In 2002, we encouraged her to go to the Kenyatta Hospital's Medical Training College to share her life story and tell the students about the disabled. It was a divine appointment. A young orthopedic technology student named Peter was sitting in the audience during her presentation. He later spent a four-month internship in the orthopedic workshop at Kijabe, where they met again. In 2006, he became Francesca's husband. You might also say he became her personal in-house orthopedic technologist!

The missionaries in Kijabe counseled her to forgive her father and the rest of her family. So she wrote her father a note and told him she forgave him because of Jesus. Eventually her father had a stroke and lost his job. To help them financially, Francesca sent 500 KSh [Kenyan shillings] every month and returned periodically to help take care of him. She also paid the school fees for her younger brothers. Eventually her father and mother (both now deceased) came to the Lord at different times of their lives, as did her immediate younger sister, three brothers and two nieces.

When BKKH partnered with Joytown Special School to provide therapy for their students, Francesca joined David Ng'ang'a and the staff in Thika. She now lives in a house on the school grounds with Peter and their young son, Jeremy. Francesca is undoubtedly one of the few ladies with spina bifida in Kenya who has delivered a child. As Children's Mentor, Francesca serves as counselor and Bible teacher. She also teaches children with spina bifida how to do CIC and care for their skin. As a result of the latter, fewer students with SB now suffer from pressure sores.

Her greatest joy and strength in her work is seeing the

children come to the Lord. Francesca, once labeled a "useless child," is now an integral part of a ministry bringing salvation and healing to the disabled in Kenya. She is instrumental in leading dozens of children to the Lord annually. She is grateful. "My disability is not a curse; it's a blessing!"

Joytown and Joyland bring many smiles to my heart. Those facilities, plus Kajiado, Dagoretti[78], and others throughout the country, are providing many services to the disabled, including surgical help, various therapies, bracing and equipment, and much-needed encouragement. But I still believe that the vast majority of disabled children in Kenya either languish at home or die too young. If Kenya is like that, then the situation is probably far worse in scores of other countries throughout Sub-Saharan Africa. I have searched my soul, prayed, and talked with others for a number of years, seeking a practical solution appropriate for today's Africa. Are there suitable training methods that can produce workers capable of meeting the many needs, particularly the surgical needs, of the majority of the disabled? I think so.

---

78 This facility is run by Feed the Children: http://www.feedthechildren.org/

RICHARD BRANSFORD

INVITATION TO AFRICA

CHAPTER 10

Dreaming for Africa's Kids

"When he saw the crowds, he had compassion for them, because they were harassed and helpless, like sheep without a shepherd."
Matthew 9:36

Often it is only in retrospect that we more fully understand the events of our lives. The "whys" of last year are answered by the "becauses" of today, as God sometimes lifts the veil to allow us a glimpse of His plan. When this happens, we can only express our humble thankfulness for giving us the privilege and opportunity to be a part of His big picture.

We can return again and again to try to analyze this through various methods, but ultimately our goal is to discern how the events of our lives – successful and unsuccessful – have fit into that plan. Even – especially! – events that I consider personal faux pas were an integral part of that plan. The unbelieving world may label such events happenstance, or chance, but I like to describe them as providential, designed by God Himself. I want to place credit where credit is due!

Looking back over 60 years, I believe the development of the work with disabled children in Africa has God's fingerprints all over it. He knew all about the disabled, their great numbers and needs, before the foundation of the earth.

In these pages, I have shared much about my life. You likely know more than you ever wished to know. However, I hope that, in spite of all of the mistakes I made, you see God's guidance and sovereignty in every step of the way.

Can we synthesize the events of the past with those of the future? What might we propose about the further development of the work with disabled children based upon the following observations?

- We know history is a marvelous teacher, and learning its lessons can prevent mankind from repeating mistakes made in previous generations.

- Most of Sub-Saharan Africa is considered to be a part of the "developing world."

- The hospitals accessed by most rural Africans in the 21st century are, in many ways, at least 50 years behind nearly all hospitals in the West.

- Due to the lack of available training, lack of state of the art equipment, and many other factors, the level of care available to most Africans is sub-standard, even in the capital cities.

- Compassionate, accessible, and/or affordable care for the poor is neither common nor a priority in nearly all developing countries.

- In general, Africa is still made up of many people groups that maintain a tribal mentality.

- Disabled children in Africa are still considered by many to be "cursed." The mothers of many disabled children are blamed for the disability. The fathers of these children usually deny responsibility and sometimes abandon their wives, leaving them to care for the children alone.

The following seem to be true for most, if not all, of Africa. The number of African specialists—physicians, surgeons, therapists, nurses, orthopedic technologists—for disabled children will be insufficient for the next 50 to 100 years for the following reasons:

- There is a tragic lack of training in Africa in the realms of neurosurgery, orthopedics, plastic surgery, and other specialties that are vitally important to the care of disabled children. The primary disabilities requiring surgical care are cleft lips/palates, hydrocephalus, spina bifida, clubfoot, burn contractures, genu varus/valgus, equinus[79], cerebral palsy, and hypospadias.

- The Dandy Africa Initiative[80], spearheaded by the Walter E. Dandy Neurosurgical Society[81], stated in 2014 that there were approximately 183,917 new cases of hydrocephalus each year in Sub-Saharan Africa (SSA). The Dandy group also suggests that there are 19 countries in SSA without any neurosurgeons, and there are only 92 neurosurgeons in 48 countries in SSA (not including South Africa and Nigeria). Whether 45,000 or 183,917 new cases of hydrocephalus, the need is huge.

- The majority of disabled children still come from

79 Usually referring to the abnormal position of the ankle with shortening of the Achilles tendon.
80 *Dandy Africa Initiative: 2nd Anniversary Message from the President.* Walter E. Dandy Neurosurgical Society, January 23, 2014.
81 http://wedns.org

desperately poor and minimally educated families.

- Physician training in Africa will appropriately continue to focus on generalists, general surgeons, gynecologists, pediatricians, and public health doctors who will have little or no training in the care of the disabled.

- National government funding streams in Africa will be inadequate to meet basic medical needs in their countries, let alone the medical needs of disabled children.

- Most schools will continue to be inaccessible for the disabled due to lack of ramps and suitable toilet facilities. There will not be a sufficient number of special schools to educate them.

- The attitude of the general public toward the disabled, plus the attitudes of the disabled toward themselves, will continue to compromise their ability to integrate into the work place or society.

- Disabled children will rarely be considered a priority in Africa.

- Providing surgical care for the disabled falls under the broader topic of the vast unmet need for all surgical services in Sub-Saharan Africa. In an August 2012 article for the New York Times entitled "Repairing the Surgery Deficit,"[82] Sarika Bansal, a journalist with an interest in international health, wrote:

"Across Africa, countless people die or become disabled because they cannot obtain necessary surgeries. It is conservatively estimated that 56 million people[83] in sub-Saharan Africa - over twice the number living

82 http://opinionator.blogs.nytimes.com/2012/08/08/repairing-the-surgery-deficit/?_r=0
83 Her numbers were taken from the Surgeons OverSeas website: https://www.surgeonsoverseas.org/

with H.I.V./AIDS - need a surgery today..."

Fifty-six million people! That's a significant gap to plug!

Recently, I re-read some letters tucked away in a binder. Dr. Michael Cotton, surgeon, author, and teacher, began a work in Zimbabwe in 1986 that continued for nearly 25 years. He wrote:

> "We have now created a group, the International Collaboration for Essential Surgery (ICES)[84] and seek to lobby for training of clinical officers to do essential surgery as defined by our manifesto in order to plug the gap. We envisage such training not to be limited to clinical officers, but also to be available to general practitioners who have not benefited from any significant surgical exposure."

How can this be done? There will simply not be a sufficient number of trained surgical specialists for a long time. Training clinical officers (CO) or medical officers (MO) to perform basic surgical procedures is called "surgical task shifting" and it is highly controversial.[85] According to the World Health Organization, task shifting involves the rational redistribution of tasks among health workforce teams. Specific tasks are moved, where appropriate, from highly qualified health workers to health workers with shorter training and fewer qualifications in order to make more efficient use of the available human resources for health."[86]

---

84 www.essentialsurgery.com
85 Chinese "barefoot doctors" (Chinese: 赤脚医生; pinyin: chìjiǎo yīshēng) have been employing this model for years. These are "farmers who received minimal basic medical and paramedical training and worked in rural villages in the People's Republic of China. Their purpose was to bring health care to rural areas where urban-trained doctors would not settle." One might say that it is likely that China did not prefer the "barefoot doctors," but they were the only option for the need at that time. https://en.wikipedia.org/wiki/Barefoot_doctor
86 http://www.who.int/healthsystems/TTR-TaskShifting.pdf

This effort has already begun. Bansal's article goes on to state:

". . . many African countries, including Zambia, Tanzania, Malawi, Mozambique and Ethiopia, have recognized the need for a more creative solution. Instead of finding ways to lure surgeons to rural areas, these countries have started experimenting with "task shifting" — that is, training non-physicians to do the basic work of surgeons."

In Zambia, surgical task shifting began in 2002 with the medical licentiate program, which trains clinical officers in basic surgeries like hernia repairs, bowel obstruction surgery, hysterectomies and more. "The real reason the program evolved was to take care of emergency surgical conditions," said James Munthali, head of surgery at University of Zambia's School of Medicine. The Surgical Society of Zambia and the Ministry of Health jointly determined the procedures in which licentiates should be trained. For instance, the program emphasizes training in cesarean sections, which constitute 45 percent of major surgeries in the country.[87]

Here is a list of 15 essential surgeries cited by 15X15 Surgery[88], agreed upon by the International Collaboration for Essential Surgery, an organization dedicated to the prioritization of global surgical care. Some of these have already been mentioned in this book:

• Neglected obstructed labor resulting in obstetric fistula

• Severe post-partum hemorrhage requiring surgical care

• Infections resulting in abscesses that require drainage

---

87 http://opinionator.blogs.nytimes.com/2012/08/08/repairing-the-surgery-deficit/?_r=0

88 http://www.essentialsurgery.com

- Severe wounds

- Severe head injury

- Airway obstruction

- Chest injury and infections

- Acute abdomen

- Fractures and dislocations

- Severe limb ischemia

- Urinary outflow obstruction

- Hernias

- Cataracts

- Clubfoot

- Cleft lip

Could the 15X15 model be revised for disabled children? Using an apprenticeship approach, surgical task shifting could focus on the development of, for lack of a better term, a "Surgical Auxiliary for the Disabled." This person might be a doctor, clinical officer, or nurse, but must be recognized in his or her own African country and granted permission to extend their skills in caring for the disabled. The trainee should have identifiable surgical skills (not necessarily provided by formal training). Each trainee can be taught in 9-12 months to perform approximately 8-10 surgical procedures:

- Ventriculoperitoneal shunt insertion

- Closure of selected spina bifidas

- Unilateral cleft lip repair

- Release of a burn contracture with flap rotation

- Full thickness and partial thickness skin grafting

- Achilles tendon lengthening

- Ponseti technique for clubfoot and posteromedial release for very selected clubfoot cases

- Depending on the exhibited skills of the trainee, the following could be possible also: osteotomies (surgical cutting or removal of bone) for genu varus/valgus and repair of selected hypospadias.

I would estimate that these operations would satisfy the surgical needs of 80-85% of disabled children. I fully believe that it could be possible to plug the surgical gap for the disabled in part through surgical task shifting. Limited, focused training in selected procedures that normally lie in the fields of plastic surgery, pediatric surgery, neurosurgery, urology, and ENT would be provided. Trainees would also be taught to recognize which patients were beyond their level of expertise and the methods for referring patients to specialists or delaying surgery until an appropriate visiting specialist was available. The Surgical Auxiliary for the Disabled might be given the option of pursuing further training in the future.

It is likely, at least for the next 20-50 years, that these rehab trainees would be capable of providing services to the disabled outside of major cities, provided that the outcomes of their procedures met established and acceptable expectations. I recognize that the outcomes of those with less training will likely not be as good as they would be if specialists provided the care. However, recent research has shown that outcomes for many basic surgeries done by well-trained and supervised clinical officers to be on par with those of the surgeons themselves.[89]

---

89 http://www.uniteforsight.org/global-health-surgery/module5

Is there a model or prototype for such a venture? The Pan African Association of Christian Surgeons (PAACS) was the dream of Dr. David Thompson who lived in Gabon, a country without a formal general surgical training program. He proposed an on-site training program for surgeons with one U.S. board-certified general surgeon residing at the hospital overseeing the program, plus scheduled teaching stints by visiting specialists. The program was to be three to four years long with periodic testing of trainees.

Initially, many quietly laughed at this unusual and ridiculous idea. But by 2011, PAACS was training 43 residents at ten hospitals across the continent. It now has 28 graduates, all of whom remain in Africa, working for underserved populations.[90] It is training African doctors at several sites and is affiliated with Loma Linda University and the Christian Medical and Dental Association (CMDA). In order to go into practice, all trainees must take and pass the qualifying exam of the College of Surgeons of East, Central and Southern Africa (COSECSA), the same exam given to university-level surgical trainees in much of Africa.

I am suggesting that a similar approach be taken to train Surgical Auxiliaries for the Disabled. The location for this training would likely be rural, but close enough to a city to allow easy access by patients, preferably on or near a main highway. Using English as the primary language would be ideal, especially if western specialists were invited to teach. Ideally, a core group of doctors committed to this training concept would reside at the site. A team of support staff such as nurses, therapists, and orthopedic technologists would be an essential part of the training program.

---

90 http://www.theatlantic.com/health/archive/2012/12/gods-surgeons-in-africa/266635/

There will be challenges, including:

- Inspiring suitable, godly doctors to commit to such an unusual training program.

- Funding such a facility, including staff salaries and medical expenses for the many poor patients found among the disabled.

- Encouraging the commitment of the trainee medical workers and their team as they may return to minimally prepared settings to care for the disabled.

- Training chaplains or spiritual workers to serve as team members, providing outreach to the disabled and to maximize the spiritual impact of this ministry.

And perhaps most importantly, the participants should have the very definite conviction that what is envisioned is from the Lord, a "Red Sea" kind of faith.

For many, especially those in the medical profession, this might sound like a dream or, for a few, a nightmare. All types of disasters can be imagined, and some, God forbid, could become realities. But, I do not believe that this is an impossible dream. To become a reality, I believe that it only awaits "chance takers," a cooperating facility, and an African nation that is unwilling to wait 50-100 years for specialists to be trained in the Western model in order to meet the current and growing needs of their disabled citizens.

Several years ago, I wandered back through some of my Bransford archives. I wrote something in 1982, probably on my Kaypro computer, using a dot matrix printer. It was pretty crude in some ways, but it contained a profound dream, or a conglomerate of dreams, that included: a primary Rehabilitation Hospital providing training, compassionate care, and specialty ministries; vocational training and pastoral/spiritual training for the unreached; camp ministries; and a string of other similar hospitals around the developing world.

Some would say that the closest I came to this dream was the Bethany Crippled Children's Centre (CURE's first hospital) and the hospitals around the world that CURE International established from that work. Some would point to Bethany Kids at Kijabe Hospital. Could it be that God used my hand, my mind, and an old Kaypro computer to begin transferring His plans to Earth? Looking at that two-dimensional drawing, colored pens and all, reveals a potentially much bigger multi-dimensional plan. Is Africa merely a starting point for what He has in mind? Obviously He knew about the 30 to 100 million disabled persons scattered all over Africa. But He likely just could not adequately communicate the extension of this work throughout the whole world to my finite human mind.

An excerpt from *The Weight of Glory* by C.S. Lewis resonates with me in regard to this dream: "…[it] pierces with such sweetness that when in very intimate conversation, the mention of it becomes imminent, we grow awkward and affect to laugh at ourselves; the secret [dream] we cannot hide and cannot tell, though we desire to do both. We cannot tell it because it is a desire for something that has never actually appeared in our experience."[91]

Those who know me well recognize that I do not hide myself as effectively as Lewis expressed. Yet, it is often difficult to try to communicate the magnitude of the dream and the inner sense that so much more can and should be done for the disabled children of the developing world.

---

91 Lewis, C. S., & Lewis, C. S. (1949). *The Weight of Glory and Other Addresses*. New York: Macmillan.

I truly am thankful for what has come to pass at CURE and BethanyKids. These are great memories, peppered with moments of disappointment, but satisfying on the whole. Yet I have a conviction – no, more than that – a certainty that He does not want us to lose sight of what remains to be done and the task He has placed before us. Millions of future disabled children and adults will display the touch of His fingerprints through our compassionate outreach. What is our role in all of this?

In 1940, Winston Churchill delivered a speech to the House of Commons that included the following phrases:

> "...we are in action at many other points in Norway and in Holland...we have to be prepared in the Mediterranean...the air battle is continuous and...many preparations ... have to be made here at home.

> I would say to the House, as I said to those who have joined this government: 'I have nothing to offer but blood, toil, tears and sweat.'

> We have before us an ordeal of the most grievous kind. We have before us many, many long months of struggle and of suffering.

> You ask, what is our aim? I can answer in one word: It is victory, victory at all costs, victory in spite of all terror, victory, however long and hard the road may be; for without victory, there is no survival."[92]

Although our war is definitely different, it is possible that we are in the midst a battle that will demand "blood, toil, tears, and sweat" as well as the effectual, fervent prayers of righteous people, for the physical and spiritual healing of multitudes of

92 http://www.winstonchurchill.org/resources/speeches/92-blood-toil-tears-and-sweat

disabled men, women, and children around the globe. If we are, we will need troops. Lots of them. And, as the old Uncle Sam poster once declared, we may even "need YOU."

MARCUS

Marcus was born September 19, 2006 in Kijabe Hospital. He had a twin sister who had no physical problems and went home with their parents. But they abandoned Marcus, diagnosed with spina bifida and hydrocephalus. A Dutch medical student, Toos Van'tVeer, took a special interest in him and frequently visited Marcus in the hospital nursery. She wrote:

"You asked if I had my eye on another abandoned baby? Yes, I do, and his name is Marculus. He has spina bifida, is paralyzed from the waist down and has hydrocephalus. He is almost four months old and was abandoned by his parents. So he still lives in the nursery, which is a very hot room. He is a big little monster among tiny babies.

"Marculus is a very happy person doing all the things a boy of his age is supposed to do, though he doesn't laugh much. He understands Dutch perfectly and we have long conversations. If I have a minute to spare you can find me in the nursery, feeding him, bathing him, changing him. I love it! Hopefully it will benefit him to have one stable person in his life. They tried to place him in an orphanage but orphanages aren't keen on taking on babies who require extra medical care.

"I would love to take him, [but] I know that wouldn't be very practical. Even so, the Kenyan law forbids a single woman to adopt a boy!"

Toos eventually would take him to her apartment when possible. Sometimes he would spend the weekend with her.

This continued for several weeks. On Sunday February 18, 2007, she wrapped him up and took him to church at RVA.

She wrote:

"Miraculously the sermon was about a faith without actions being a dead faith, and the pastor asked if anybody knew of a case where they would like to help but didn't know how. I saw my chance!!! So I got up and went to the front of the church and told Marculus' story through a microphone (scary things), and I said he needed a home. Afterwards during prayer the little boy began to talk in his own way but I thought, Let him be, let people know he is here! After the service a very friendly Canadian couple came up to me and said they would think about taking him!"

That Canadian couple was Nora Lynn and Wayne Hogman. They had a daughter at RVA and had frequently come to visit her. Now they took Marculus to their apartment and soon fell in love with this little one. They lived in RVA housing, the Kijabe Motel, hospital housing, Moffat housing, and in Nairobi at Mayfield—wherever they could— as they initiated adoption proceedings and waited for that process to run its course. Meanwhile, they chose to change his name from Marculus to Marcus.

In every place they stayed, Marcus made many friends from all over the world. Marcus had a "smile that was contagious" and was an "ambassador of hope" in the spina bifida ward at Kijabe Hospital and nearly everywhere he went. Mamas who saw him "dared to hope that one day their own child[ren] might be as alert and cheerful as he was."

Marcus, the Hogmans, and David Muhota, Marcus' guardian ad litem, went to court on several occasions seeking to finalize an adoption. On November 14, 2008, Marcus and the Hogmans went to their final court appearance for the adoption. They were devastated to learn that the adoption was not going to be approved. Heartbroken, they had to give him up.

Ian Castleman Orphanage soon opened their arms to Marcus and he went to live there on Friday, November 30, 2008. He had a happy two weeks there, once again gathering friends around him. But on Monday December 15, 2008, at 2 years, 2 months, and 26 days old, Marcus developed a fever.

The orphanage took him to the Valley Hospital in Nakuru

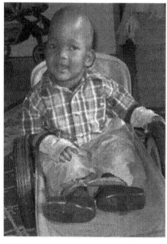

where he was treated with antibiotics, but they didn't seem to help. Marcus died peacefully later that night. The cause of death was felt to be meningitis. This was likely complicated by his shunt.

The Hogmans were not in Kenya at the time of Marcus' death. They wrote: "We heard early this morning of the death of our sweet baby, Marcus. We know that every possible measure was taken and we are

Marcus

comforted with the knowledge that he is in the arms of Jesus right now. I'm sure he is trying out his new legs and is singing at the top of his lungs...praises to our wonderful Heavenly Father, while we sit here and cry. That's okay with me, but it sure hurts!

"I was wondering if there is any way that Marcus could be buried in Kijabe? I realize the distance is long [from Nakuru to Kijabe] and the expenses might be great. We are willing to send the money but we know that that might be the easy part. Marcus' "people" are all in Kijabe. His many aunties, uncles, grandparents and friends who surrounded him throughout his short life live in Kijabe. How we wish we could be there, but if there could be a funeral for him in Kijabe and if he could be buried in that cemetery it would be a comfort to us. In Kenya I know that it is important that the deceased person be buried in his "home" and now I understand why. If my request is not possible, we will go with what is best."

Marcus was, indeed, buried at Kijabe. I wrote this in a prayer letter on December 21, 2008: "I shared with you and many others about the death of Marcus. David Muhota was at the funeral. He shared about Marcus' effect on his life. It was interesting to see an adult Kenyan break down and cry as he spoke about Marcus. In Kenya, one seldom sees a man cry, but Marcus had truly touched many of us. David seemed moved to try to do more to improve the terrible state of the Kenyan justice system when it comes to adoption.

It was also revealing to see the real mixture of people who came for the burial. There were probably 50-60 there. A Kenyan lady had dressed Marcus for burial, and two Kenyan men carried the small casket over to the cemetery from the morgue. Both Africans and expats had been touched by Marcus' life. The casket was lowered into the ground and each person came forth with a rose to place on top of the casket. It was a serious, sad time, but it too was a time of rejoicing for Marcus."

Could Marcus have been saved with better, more comprehensive medical care in Kenya? Could Marcus have had a better chance to live if the court had allowed his adoption and he had gone to Canada? We don't know. But what we do know is that Marcus' short little life had a big impact. He was a true blessing to many, many people and inspired some to make a greater effort to improve services, both legal and medical, for disabled children in Africa. He will never be forgotten.

REBECCA OPETSI

Social Worker, Signposts Ministries[93] and YWAM[94], Tanzania

Rebecca Opetsi was born in western Kenya. Her parents recognized the "big wound" on her back and her clubfeet. People tried to discourage her mother from trying to get help and told her that children with such a wound die young. Rebecca's mother was a believer and would not accept that.

Rebecca was brought to Kijabe when she was about three months old. We were able to surgically close her back. When she was nine months old, her family moved to Nairobi. Eventually, Rebecca was able to walk but somewhat awkwardly. She lacked sensation in her feet.

In Nairobi, they met a woman who had received clubfoot surgery at Kijabe Hospital. She encouraged them to bring Rebecca back to Kijabe for additional operations for her clubfeet.

As Rebecca grew, her incontinence became increasingly unmanageable and more and more of a social stigma. Compounding the problem, uninformed and unsympathetic teachers thought that either she was faking her condition or that it might be contagious. They even eliminated her from a singing competition and, at one point, expelled her from school because of her disability.

When she was 11 years old, her parents took her back to

93 http://signpostsministries.org/
94 http://www.ywam.org/

Kijabe for training in CIC and further corrective surgery on her foot. But even by age 13, her foot was still not okay. So off they went to Kijabe again. This time the surgery went well, but she developed "compartment syndrome" that blocked the circulation in her leg and caused the tissues to die. This necessitated the amputation of her leg. When she was satisfactorily healed, she was fitted with an artificial leg.

Fortunately for Rebecca, Francesca Maina[95], herself an amputee with spina bifida, was then working at Kijabe. She counseled Rebecca from her own life story and helped her through that very difficult time.

Rebecca finished primary school and I wrote a recommendation letter for her admission to Joytown Secondary School. She says that living there was "a great eye-opener" for her. She met children without hands who could draw by holding a pencil with their feet or mouths. "I found myself helping other people. I was able to participate in extracurricular activities like swimming and singing in the school choir, wheelchair basketball, poetry class. I did so much!"

After graduation and a short IT course, she secured a scholarship at Tangos College, the Catholic university of Eastern Africa. It was a 50/50 scholarship. Rebecca didn't know where she would come up with the half of the tuition for which she was responsible. But a Canadian woman she met at a conference sponsored by the International Federation of Spina Bifida and Hydrocephalus, stepped forward and paid the remaining 50% for all three years of school. She received a Bachelor's degree in Sustainable Human Development.

She volunteered with BK for several months and then I put her in touch with Dr. Pamela Follett who was starting

95 See Chapter 9.

an outreach to the disabled in Tanzania. Soon thereafter, Rebecca moved to YWAM's "base in the bush," just south of Dar es Salaam. After a six-month orientation in the Discipleship Training School, she began traveling to churches and villages where she sought to locate disabled children and secure medical care and educational opportunities for them. She has found over 150 children so far.

Rebecca Opetsi

The top five disabilities she sees are cerebral palsy, hydrocephalus, spina bifida, muscular dystrophy, and clubfoot. Her biggest frustration has been locating a place where they can get surgical care.

Recently, she had a heartbreaking case. She located a baby with SB/HC named Neema (Grace). She sent her and her mother to the national hospital in Dar where they were told over and over again to "come next month." Neema got weaker and weaker. Finally, Rebecca personally took her to the hospital. She tried to be very assertive, telling the staff that Neema was not in good condition and needed help right away. The staff admitted her. But sadly, after Rebecca left, they immediately discharged her. On the way home from the hospital, Neema died on her mother's lap.

Rebecca works alone, but would love to have a team to help her. Her ideal team would include a doctor dedicated to helping disabled children, a nurse, a physical therapist, and a teacher. Together they could provide an integrated approach to care for the needs of the children she finds. She also has a strong interest in legal advocacy for the disabled.

Rebecca is somewhat of a fanatic when it comes to disabled children. She recognizes that the needs of the disabled are huge, all over the developing world. She urges people to join the work and says there's a job for everyone who wants to be involved. "If you come to help, you'll be able to touch lives in a greater way and realize how much you can do!"

KEVIN DEMARS

The DeMars family lived near us in Kijabe, Kenya. Brian coached my sons in basketball. Brian and Gaylene already had one son, Matthew. I became Gaylene's obstetrician for baby #2, Krista, whom I delivered by Caesarian section on my own birthday. As Krista grew up she would either call me or send me an email every year to wish me, "Happy Birthday!" That was very special.

Another pregnancy followed and one evening Gaylene went into labor. She had been advised to have another C-section. Gaylene's mother and Brian were there for the big occasion. They asked if they could come into the operating room to see this great event and I agreed.

I began what was presumed to be a routine, repeat C-section. A midwife was in the room to take the baby, and, if need be, resuscitate him or her. The anesthetist also stood ready to help. I made the incision through the skin and entered the thinned uterus. The baby's head was disengaged from the pelvis and I brought out a crying little boy named Kevin.

Except all was not what had been anticipated. All was not well. As I handed him to the midwife, my heart sank. Kevin had a bilateral cleft lip and a large cleft palate. His grandmother and father stood staring, wondering. There was nothing I could say at that point. Usually this would be a time of laughing and talking, but everyone was silent. Kevin was breathing and physiologically seemed to be doing well, but his facial condition was overwhelming.

I finished the operation and I tried to evaluate how I could support this family. They were on an unfamiliar road now. Initially there would be the problem of feeding Kevin, a job that would take an immense amount of patience. Fortunately, for some unknown reason, I had a small supply of special nipples just for this purpose at my home.

Kevin did gain weight, and eventually the family returned to the United States where they not only had a supportive nuclear family but also a team of medical specialists who planned and carried out the necessary care.

They subsequently returned to Kijabe and lived there for several more years while making intermittent visits to the U.S. for additional care. God called a speech therapist and orthodontist to Kijabe, for the first time in the school's history, to provide the care Kevin needed.

At the beginning it was tough, but Kevin flourished in the small close-knit community where he was an accepted and much-loved child. His joyfulness in life was a blessing that he shared with others.

Gaylene would come to Kijabe Hospital or BCCC when

special medical teams arrived to repair cleft lips and palates. She and Kevin sat with distraught mothers whose infants suffered conditions similar to Kevin's. She could realistically say to these mothers, "I understand!" She was thankful that God could use Kevin's story to encourage others.

Kevin's family settled in the U.S. when he was nine years old. It was not easy growing up in a culture that emphasizes physical looks. Probably because of this dichotomy, Kevin recognizes that a person's inner spirit is worth more than their outer looks. He has a heart for those who struggle. This was demonstrated during his U.S. school days by standing up for the little guy being bullied.

The name "Kevin" means "gentle and kind" and he really does live up to his name!

Kevin's delivery occurred over 25 years ago. The last time I saw him, he was a handsome young man with a healthy sense of personal worth. Gaylene, Brian, Krista, Kevin, and I looked at each other knowingly and marveled over God's goodness.

CHAPTER 11

Pushing Ahead and Challenging You

"And whoever gives one of these little ones even a cup of cold water because he is a disciple, truly, I say to you, he will by no means lose his reward." Matthew 10:42

Millie and I have been happily married for over 50 years. We spent 35 of those years in Africa. Kenya is home for our seven children. In a sense we experience constant "déjà vu" with some of our kids on "the field," some in medicine, some in ministry, and some with African roots. Our five older kids are also happily married and have provided us with 17 grand-children. Joshua and Philip are growing into young men, and we are thrilled that they became Bransfords.

Millie, Philip, and I live in a neat house on top of a hill in Boone, NC, with a beautiful panoramic view. When the ice and snow arrive the roads are treacherous, but we have the privilege of looking out onto a winter wonderland that reminds me of that first pristine snow I experienced in Baltimore so many years ago. While there are attractive elements in retiring, especially reading the books that entice me, those things do not satisfy the passion generated by playing an active role in the lives of disabled children.

It is October 1, 2015, and I am in my office at home. It is foggy outside. I can only see a short distance. The same is true for the future of the ideas proposed in this book...I can only see a short way. But in my mind the images of Francesca, Gladys, Rebecca, Kevin, Daisy, Michael, Sophy, Annie, Anthony, Fazira, Marcus, Philip, and many others are absolutely clear. They are all my cheerleaders. Four of those mentioned are dead. One is likely dying. Maybe, in some non-theological way, those already in Heaven are tapping God on the shoulder daily to remind Him not to forget the disabled children of the developing world. Maybe they are asking Him to remind me not to give up dreaming "the impossible dream."

I have not given up. To paraphrase Martin Luther King, Jr., "I still have a dream." We can meet the needs of disabled children throughout Africa. I really felt that we could assimilate a team, develop appropriate training, and go into every country in Africa that did not have a sufficient plan to meet the needs of their disabled. And I was arrogant enough to think God would provide sufficiently to bring it about, that He might possibly sell His "cattle on a thousand hills" for my children, His children, to fulfill this dream. I think He is sitting up on His throne, intensely pleased that some are prepared to dream this dream, a dream big enough to reflect His glory.

So what would my dream be for the next 20 years of my life? (There's a good chance I'll live that long: my Dad died at 96 and my grandmother at 98.) I envision a task-shifting training facility with 50-75 beds dedicated to the work with disabled children. I would prefer to see the program associated with an established hospital that is already seeking to bring glory to God. As I wrote in Chapter 6, "…the envisioned work with the disabled also needed to dwell within an organization big enough to cooperate with other entities while maintaining its own unique identity."

Dwell on that sentence. I think that in the end it is really important. Can that degree of autonomy and identity be accomplished within an existing organization without becoming a threat to the mother institution? I believe so, but it would take an effort and lots of understanding on the part of both organizations. Jealousies must be avoided. Respect for the God-endowed missions of each endeavor must be maintained. And the objective of both entities must be to glorify God.

I imagine the first training facility would initially be in Tanzania, Kenya, or Uganda. I hope two trainees for the surgical stream could be added every three months, with a total training period of 9-12 months. The ideal would be two trainees from each referring institution, thereby encouraging

Dick with former patients and friends at retirement party in 2011

companionship in the work. One will always be on the job while the other is away. This arrangement helps relieve anxiety and guilt, allowing workers to truly relax and rejuvenate during their vacations, which is vitally important.

My dream also includes a nurse, operating room technician, therapist, and chaplain from each feeder institution receiving 4-6 weeks of special training at the training facility to complete the team.

If I try to gaze even further down this foggy road, I envision that such a training facility could be duplicated in other locations in the developing world. Though my heart has been in Africa for 35 years, I want more of God's heart for all the disabled of this world.

I am also going to assume that God's first priority is not perfect bodies. Yes, I think that He does ache for broken bodies, especially little broken bodies. But I believe His first desire is to receive contrite souls that love Him and own Him as their Lord and Savior and the God of the entire universe. What about the souls of men and women, boys and girls, and babies? What if our work were present throughout Africa and as a result, we could see millions of boys and girls, moms and dads, and others come to a saving knowledge of Jesus Christ – unreached people groups of all kinds. I anticipate that one day I will rest in peace with God and be met by many formerly disabled children, helped by our ministry in this life and made whole in the next life, who have preceded me into Paradise.

Throughout my career I have learned several things. I have finally admitted to myself and to others that I am a better starter than a finisher. I am a visionary often with good ideas but I don't have the administrative skills to effectively follow through and accomplish those ideas. I definitely need others to make the dream a reality.

Part of the conundrum is that many places in the developing world have discussed task shifting, but only a few have implemented it with significant effectiveness. Task shifting to create more medical expertise in the realm of general surgery, such as routine surgical emergencies, is poorly regarded, especially by many of the medical experts in the capital cities of Africa. Task shifting for the disabled hasn't even made it off of the proverbial drawing board. The few already involved in the surgical care of the disabled are specialists, often with extra training. They meet only a fraction of the needs of the disabled. Most cannot imagine sharing this work with non-physicians or non-specialists.

When I have naively questioned medical colleagues for their ideas about how we might approach the enormous task of helping 45,000 to 184,000 children each year with hydrocephalus alone, there is an uncomfortable silence. Perhaps it is a mutual feeling of guilt for not having any plan at all, no matter how wild it might seem. Task shifting is very threatening to most. It is even a bit frightening to me. However, I sincerely think that it can work. It must work, for there is no alternative, at least for the next 50-100 years!

I am continuing to seek opportunities to promote this radical idea. Scott Taylor, longtime friend and former Air Force pilot, introduced me to Joe Schmidt, founder of the Audacity Factory.[96] Audacity Factory is a think tank that brings visionaries like me together with people who are better acquainted, motivated, and capable of organizing a task and getting it done. In general, they are not medical people and largely rely on others for medical advice and information. But they under-

96 http://www.audacityfactory.com/

stand how to develop and implement a business model.

Is our idea of task shifting moving along? I think we are taking positive steps in the right direction. A business plan may not yet be on paper, but a few members of the Audacity Factory are considering its elements. A summit to discuss the idea with an expanded think tank is anticipated in the future.

I have also talked with the board of Signposts Ministries.[97] Its objective is to assist families with disabled children in the U.S. Recently, they have expanded their vision and have a ministry to the disabled in Tanzania[98]. We are learning a lot about each other. I've also met with some of the leaders of SIM[99] and have learned a lot from them as well.

The vast need hovers like a storm cloud over the continent of Africa. A successful marriage with another organization to meet this need has yet to be accomplished. I feel some urgency to arrange that marriage and get on with the project. I hope cooperation with other organizations will occur. Actually, it must occur.

Many years ago my friend Dick Brogden wrote this allegory[100] to express his deep sadness over the apathy and lack of workers in a desperately needy world. Each year I re-read it several times. I can fully identify with the frustration and confusion it describes. Perhaps it will similarly impact you.

"In a distant land of the decaying I happened upon a hospital. There were many pseudo-hospitals, clinics, and traditional healers scattered in the shadow of its mighty walls but a quick inspection proved them dirty and inad-

97 http://signpostsministries.org/
98 See profile for Rebecca Opetsi.
99 http://www.sim.org/
100 Reprinted with permission from the author.

equate. I made my way into the hospital via a back door and climbed the stairwell to the top floor. I pushed open the door to the children's ward and was repulsed by the smell. Children were crowded three to a crib. Few if any of them were diapered, and it was obvious that they had wallowed in their own filth for some time. A cacophony of desperate tears erupted at my entrance. Infants with open lesions lifted their hands in desperate appeal. Others could not muster the strength to stretch forth their weakened limbs and simply stared dully.

I realized that I needed to find the medical staff quickly and ran out of the room in order to do so. Leaping down the stairs three at a time I raced to the ward on the floor below me. I rushed in only to be stopped suddenly by silence. The ward seemed to stretch interminably. Row after row of the aged stretched out like merging railroad tracks in the distance. They lay there mute and hopeless. On the horizon of that hall I thought I could see a solitary physician, but I would not swear to it if under oath. I numbly spun on my heel and continued my search for doctors. On floor after floor as I descended that building I entered wards that were bursting with the ill and wounded and largely absent of their healers. The horribly burned, maimed, and suffering tossed listlessly on filthy sheets vainly waiting for medicine, comfort, or cleaning.

I finally arrived at the ground floor, my pace slowed to a walk by a mounting sense of despair. As I pushed open the ward door I was smacked in the face by beauty. Fragrant smells wafted from freshly arranged flowers. Soothing music slipped from hidden speakers. The floor gleamed as if recently polished, bright sunshine beamed in the picture windows.

Hospital beds contained patrons smiling in comfort. It was obvious that some were in critical condition and yet others seemed to have minor abrasions or slight temperatures. The puzzling thing about the ward however was its activity. Hoards of doctors raced around that ward like frenzied termites. Nurses, technicians, and medical assistants jockeyed for elbowroom around each bed. As new patients trickled in they were practically devoured by aggressive physicians, desperately trying to pull them to the empty bed of their responsibility. Patients seemed overmedicated and triple bandaged.

I stopped a physician who was hurtling by me to join a throng of thirty gathered around one young man who had cut himself shaving.

"Please, could you come with me?" I asked. "There are desperately sick patients on the upper floors!"

"I would love to," he replied. "But I have not been called to those floors." Another doctor bumped into me as she vainly tried to join a team who were arguing about who would get to operate on an ingrown fingernail.

"Please Ma'am, it is urgent that we have more doctors upstairs," I pleaded.

She scalded me with her eyes, "Can you not see that there are sick people here as well?" I could, of course, and I was not suggesting that all the doctors transfer, but couldn't one or two?

I drifted towards another bustling group who were gathered around a pleasant man who was explaining just how he would like his tummy tightened.

"Excuse me, sir," I asked one of the short doctors who was struggling to see over the shoulders of those in front of him, "Could you possibly come help out on a needy floor?"

He winced a little and then muttered, "You know I wish I could, but I am not cut out for that kind of stuff. I am glad you can do it, but...well...you know...I just can't." And he scuttled off to join a dozen doctors who were reading the chart of a nearby soul.

I tried several more times but was continually rebuffed. Every reason had a measure of truth. Every reason went further to ensure that those struggling for life on the floors above us would certainly die.

I climbed slowly back up the stairs. The music receded, the lovely fragrance faded. The hustle and bustle of clean, intelligent, capable doctors faded into the silence of desperation. I walked with a heavy heart down the silent halls of the neglected. I could not understand it. I paused to hold the hand of a sufferer, and my tears joined his in anguished refrain. He took one last fragile breath. His eyes framed one last question. And then he passed into the ranks of the damned."

All of us are confronted by situations that demand decisions. The impact of our decisions may not be evident for decades. What are those critical decisions that determine so much about the lives that we live? And how many Elijahs will come into our lives to prepare us for the pathway we will embark upon? And what will be the professional, spiritual, relational events that will color our walk through life? Are we willing to take risks when it comes to the important things in life? What is really important?

As I contemplate this, I'm reminded of my visits to Kakuma Refugee Camp in northern Kenya. This camp held 85,000 refugees in a very rustic desert setting. Bore holes supplied water, fire wood and food was trucked in, schooling was available through high school, and medical care was rudimentary at best, generally provided by well-meaning Kenyans and refugees. Most of the refugees were Sudanese, but there were others from Somalia, Ethiopia, DRC, and Rwanda. Some were recent arrivals, and some had been there for 15-20 years.

I went there intermittently to evaluate disabled children. The community-based refugee rehab team pre-screened patients and brought them to clinic sites around the camp for our visit. After patients were selected and scheduled for operations, the task of getting them to Kijabe involved an arduous day and a half trip by road, first through the desert at night when marauding bandits were less likely to attack, and then down to Kijabe on Kenya's main highway.

One trip to this camp was particularly memorable. We left Kijabe in the dark at 5:30 AM and arrived at Wilson Airport about 7 AM. The plane was ready, but the sky threatened rain. Denny, our pilot, loaded the plane and meandered around checking this and that, but he kept looking up at the sky. Although I am sure he was not completely comfortable, he said that we could proceed while warning us that we might be forced to turn back.

The takeoff was smooth, but then Denny began weaving his way between ominous clouds, up and down and back and forth, seeking a safe flight path. We could tell he was nervous. We passed Naivasha, and then muddy Lake Baringo was lost from sight. The swaying movement of the plane weaving between storm clouds lulled me to sleep.

The next thing I remember was a sudden rousing comment, "Look for a place where we can set the plane down!" It was an "All hands on deck!" type of command. Each of us went to our battle stations. He told us that even a road would do. We spotted one, but it really wasn't much of a road. Then we saw a dry riverbed. But it wasn't dry for long; we watched as a massive wall of water surged through it. The plane kept circling lower and lower, and then, of all things, we saw an actual small dirt strip beside a miniscule village.

Denny had never landed on this strip before. Pilots usually use strips that have already been used by others from their team, but not this time. There really was no choice.

We had a bumpy, but safe, landing. The storm soon burst upon us, bringing such torrential rain that even the goats sought shelter under the wings of the plane. After 20-30 minutes, it was over. The sun came out, and we walked the strip, filling in small depressions made by rivulets of water to make the strip somewhat smoother for take off. After boarding, we bounced down the runway and resumed our flight to Kakuma.

Though still cloudy, the weather to the north seemed far less threatening. The storm had come and gone. We safely arrived in Kakuma about three hours later than planned. And, although we had to work late and extra hard, we were happy to be alive.

There are no "emergency dirt strips" for the disabled in Africa. They have to weather the storm in any way they can. Many never find a road or a strip in the form of a hospital or a doctor where they can take shelter from the storm. Many just don't make it.

Our ambition, medically speaking, is to provide a safe landing for those caught in the storm. Paul captures it well in Philippians 3:12-14 (NIV):

> *"Not that I have already obtained all this, or have already arrived at my goal, but I press on to take hold of that for which Christ Jesus took hold of me. Brothers and sisters, I do not consider myself yet to have taken hold of it. But one thing I do: Forgetting what is behind and straining toward what is ahead, I press on toward the goal to win the prize for which God has called me heavenward in Christ Jesus."*

Paul would have been a fantastic fighter pilot. If I had been in his formation, I would have thrilled to know that he was my wingman.

When we flew in Africa we were exposed to all kinds of risks. Similarly, as we pursue a dream to alleviate desperate need, the flight path will be uncertain. But we, His adopted children, can rest assured that He will go with us through the storms. We have the privilege of serving the Almighty God. We are His children. Somehow – and I do not fully understand it – while we worship Him, He adores us. He adores us enough to entrust us with a portion of His heart and His dreams for disabled children. In this relationship we must not be content to pursue anything less than His very best. The Master Designer desires to make something beautiful of every life that is yielded to Him. Second Chroniclea 16:9 states,

> *"For the eyes of the Lord run to and fro throughout the whole earth, to give strong support to those whose heart is blameless toward him."*

Paul, in Romans 12:1-2, reminds us:

> *"Therefore I urge you, brethren, by the mercies of God, to present your bodies a living and holy sacrifice, acceptable to God, which is your spiritual service of worship. And do not be conformed to this world, but be transformed by the renewing of your mind, so that you may prove what the will of God is, that which is good and acceptable and perfect."*

My conviction is that God's desire, His will, is to improve the quality of life of the disabled, His little ones, while also speaking of Jesus and His words of eternal life into their lives and the lives of those around them. As I gaze out at the horizon of opportunity, I truly believe that this ministry – this dream of mine –will touch the physical and spiritual lives of millions in the developing world. I humbly invite you to be a part of it.

Epilogue

DAISY

Kijabe, Kenya
September 10, 2009

In the last few months, Daisy had repeated complications from her shunt. CTs of the head demonstrated that the brain had truly expanded, but the size of her ventricles had likely been enlarged since she was young. A new shunt was inserted, but it leaked. The pressure in her head increased again, and subsequently the shunt became infected.

Through all of these tragedies, Daisy did not seem to grow discouraged, and she continued to try to encourage others, including me. She was a happy, joyful little girl who brought her own brand of sunshine into the lives of everyone around her. In late August, she was admitted with the shunt track infection and grew weaker and weaker. She was on the best antibiotics we had and her infected wound was being dressed daily.

At one point, Daisy told her mother, Emma, that she saw a bright light and thought that somebody was shining a very bright torch (flashlight) at her. But there was no torch and Emma did not see the light Daisy saw. Daisy slipped into a coma. One morning, a patient died in the bed next to her, causing the patient's family to cry out in grief. When they shouted, Daisy suddenly woke from her coma and asked her mother why people were shouting.

Then she slipped back into unresponsiveness. I discussed her deteriorating condition with Emma. She understood that the outlook was not good.

Today, Daisy entered Heaven. I am sure that she will receive the crown that she has rightly earned. No longer will it have to be an oversized crown, for she will be beautiful in the eyes of the King there. You know a lot about my concept of Heaven and my special kids. When we, who have been blessed with a normal body, get to the heavenly gates, we will have to wait. My kids will be able to run and jump and laugh as they run in ahead of us.

And do you know what? When I enter, Princess Daisy will be there to welcome me and take my hand.

Appendix

The Road Not Taken

Robert Frost

Two roads diverged in a yellow wood,
And sorry I could not travel both
And be one traveler, long I stood
And looked down one as far as I could
To where it bent in the undergrowth;

Then took the other, as just as fair,
And having perhaps the better claim,
Because it was grassy and wanted wear;
Though, as for that, the passing there
Had worn them really about the same,

And both that morning equally lay
In leaves no step had trodden black.
Oh, I kept the first for another day!
Yet knowing how way leads on to way,
I doubted if I should ever come back.

I shall be telling this with a sigh
Somewhere ages and ages hence:
Two roads diverged in a wood, and I –
I took the one less traveled by,
And that has made all the difference.

Take My Life, and Let It Be[101]

Frances R. Havergal

Take my life and let it be
consecrated, Lord, to thee.
Take my moments and my days;
let them flow in endless praise,
let them flow in endless praise.

Take my hands and let them move
at the impulse of thy love.
Take my feet and let them be
swift and beautiful for thee,
swift and beautiful for thee.

Take my voice and let me sing
always, only, for my King.
Take my lips and let them be
filled with messages from thee,
filled with messages from thee.

Take my silver and my gold;
not a mite would I withhold.
Take my intellect and use
every power as thou shalt choose,
every power as thou shalt choose.

Take my will and make it thine;
it shall be no longer mine.
Take my heart it is thine own;
it shall be thy royal throne,
it shall be thy royal throne.

Take my love; my Lord, I pour

---

101 http://www.hymnary.org/text/take_my_life_and_let_it_be

at thy feet its treasure store.
Take myself, and I will be
ever, only, all for thee,
ever, only, all for thee.

A Prayer for the Children[102]

Ina J. Hughes

We pray for the children...

who put chocolate everywhere,
who like to be tickled,
who stomp in puddles and ruin their new pants,
who sneak popsicles before supper,
who erase holes in math workbooks,
who can never find their shoes.

And we pray for those...

who stare at photographers from behind barbed wire,
who can't bound down the street in a new pair of sneakers,
who never "counted potatoes,"
who are born in places where we wouldn't be caught dead,
who will never go to the circus,
who live in an X-rated world.

We pray for children...

who bring us sticky kisses and fistfuls of dandelions,
who sleep with the dog and bury goldfish,
who hug us in a hurry and forget their lunch money,
who cover themselves with Band-aids and sing off key,
who squeeze toothpaste all over the sink,
who slurp their soup.

---

102 http://www.heartlight.org/feature/sf_980715_children.html

And we pray for those...

who never get dessert,
who have no safe blanket to drag behind them,
who watch their parents watch them die,
who can't find any bread to steal,
who don't have any rooms to clean up,
whose pictures aren't on anybody's dresser,
whose monsters are real.

We pray for children...

who spend all their allowance before Tuesday,
who throw tantrums in the grocery store and pick at their food,
who like ghost stories,
who shove dirty clothes under the bed,
who never rinse out the tub,
who get visits from the tooth fairy,
who don't like to be kissed in front of the carpool,
who squirm in church or temple and scream on the phone,
whose tears we sometimes laugh at and whose smiles can
make us cry.

And we pray for those...

whose nightmares come in the daytime,
who will eat anything,
who have never seen a dentist,
who aren't spoiled by anybody,
who go to bed hungry and cry themselves to sleep,
who live and move, but have no being.

We pray for children...

who want to be carried and for those who must,
who we never give up on
and for those who don't get a second chance.

TAKE TWO HEARTS

For those we smother and . . .
for those who will grab the hand of anybody kind enough to
offer it.

Prayers of the Bransford Family

We invented many kinds of prayers when the kids in our
home were young. The most memorable were the "Fisherman"
prayers when we would each think of someone unsaved and
pray that they would come to know the Savior. "Wiseman"
prayers occurred when we would all kneel to pray in adora-
tion to our Lord, as the magi did when they found the baby
Jesus. "Pop Up" prayers happened when we all sat together
around the room and the one who wished to pray would jump
out of his or her seat to do so. "Thank You" and "Praise" prayers
are self-explanatory, as are regular prayers, giving each the opportunity to pray about whatever was on his or her heart for
however long he or she wanted. Sometimes the one who was
in charge that day would just ask for certain ones to pray instead of having everybody pray. Each child had designated
days when he or she prayed for each meal and was in charge
of directing the prayers for the evening devotions.

Having seven kids made it easy to divide up the seven days.
Each one had a "prayer day" when he or she received lots of
specific prayer. This continued even after they left our home
and established families of their own. Sunday is Kat's (Susie's)
day, Monday is Bethany's day, Tuesday is Chris' day, Wednesday is Josh's day, Thursday is Jon's day, Friday is Philip's day,
and Saturday is Rick's day. Prior to Josh and Philip joining our
family, Wednesday was "Dad's" day and Friday was "Mom's."
Now we just ask the family to think of Mom and Dad every
day!

RICHARD BRANSFORD

A Reading List

In addition to the footnoted resources, here is a short list of recently published articles about surgical needs in the developing world, essential surgeries, and surgical task shifting. Articles are listed in alphabetical order according to primary author's last name. Direct links are provided for some, but all can be accessed at: http://www.worldcat.org/

Beard, Jessica H., Lawrence B. Oresanya, Larry Akoko, Ally Mwanga, Charles A. Mkony, and Rochelle A. Dicker. 2014. "Surgical Task-Shifting in a Low-Resource Setting: Outcomes After Major Surgery Performed by Nonphysician Clinicians in Tanzania." *World Journal of Surgery: Official Journal of the International Society of Surgery/ Société Internationale De Chirurgie.* 38 (6): 1398-1404.

Bergström S. 2005. "Who will do the caesareans when there is no doctor? Finding creative solutions to the human resource crisis". *BJOG: an International Journal of Obstetrics and Gynaecology.* 112 (9): 1168-9.

Blanchard, R. 2001. "Training to serve unmet surgical needs worldwide." *Journal of the American College of Surgeons.* 193 (4): 417-427.

Choo S, H Perry, AA Hesse, F Abantanga, E Sory, H Osen, CW McCord, and F Abdullah. 2011. "Surgical training and experience of medical officers in Ghana's district hospitals." *Academic Medicine: Journal of the Association of American Medical Colleges.* 86 (4): 529-33.

Chu K. 2009. "General surgeons: a dying breed?" *Archives of Surgery (Chicago, Ill.: 1960).* 144 (6): 498-9.

Chu K, P Rosseel, P Gielis, and N Ford. 2009. "Surgical task shifting in Sub-Saharan Africa". *PLoS Medicine.* 6 (5).

Chu, Kathryn M, Ford, Nathan P, and Trelles, Miguel. 2011. "Providing surgical care in Somalia: A model of task shifting". BioMed

Central Ltd. http://www.conflictandhealth.com/content/5/1/12.

Cumbi, Amelia, Pereira, Caetano, Malalane, Raimundo, Vaz, Fernando, McCord, Colin, Bacci, Alberta, and Bergström, Staffan. n.d. *Major surgery delegation to mid-level health practitioners in Mozambique: health professionals' perceptions.* BioMed Central. http://www. pubmedcentral.nih.gov/articlerender.fcgi?artid=2235883.

Curci M. 2012. "Task shifting overcomes the limitations of volunteerism in developing nations." *Bulletin of the American College of Surgeons.* 97 (10): 9-14.

De Brouwere, V and Dieng, T and Diadhiou, M and Witter, Sophie and Denerville, E (2009) Task Shifting for Emergency Obstetric Surgery in District Hospitals in Senegal. *Reproductive Health Matters, Volume (33).* Pp. 32-44. ISSN 09688080. Elsevier. http://eresearch.qmu. ac.uk/2705/1/Task_shifting.pdf.

Galukande, Moses, Kaggwa, Sam, Sekimpi, Patrick, Kakaire, Othman, Katamba, Achilles, Munabi, Ian, Runumi, Francis Mwesigye, et al. 2013. *Use of surgical task shifting to scale up essential surgical services: a feasibility analysis at facility level in Uganda.* BioMed Central. http:// www.ncbi.nlm.nih.gov/pmc/articles/PMC3734124/

Gosselin, Richard A., Gyamfi, Yaw-Adu, and Contini, Sandro. n.d. *Challenges of Meeting Surgical Needs in the Developing World.* Springer-Verlag. http://www.ncbi.nlm.nih.gov/pmc/articles/PMC3017318/

Henry, Jaymie Ang, Chris Bem, Caris Grimes, Eric Borgstein, Nyengo Mkandawire, William E. G. Thomas, S. William A. Gunn, Robert H. S. Lane, and Michael H. Cotton. 2015. „Essential Surgery: The Way Forward." *World Journal of Surgery: Official Journal of the International Society of Surgery/Société Internationale De Chirurgie* 39 (4): 822-832.

Lehmann, Uta, Van Damme, Wim, Barten, Francoise, and Sanders, David. 2009. *Task shifting: the answer to the human resources crisis in Africa?* BioMed Central Ltd. BioMed Central Ltd. http://www.human-resources-health.com/content/7/1/49.

Loutfi A, AP McLean, and J Pickering. 1995. "Training general practitioners in surgical and obstetrical emergencies in Ethiopia."

Tropical Doctor. 25: 22-6.

Luboga, Sam, Macfarlane, Sarah B., von Schreeb, Johan, Kruk, Margaret E., Cherian, Meena N., Bergström, Staffan, Bossyns, Paul B. M., et al. 2009. *Increasing Access to Surgical Services in Sub-Saharan Africa: Priorities for National and International Agencies Recommended by the Bellagio Essential Surgery Group.* Public Library of Science. http://www.ncbi.nlm.nih.gov/pmc/articles/PMC2791210.

McQueen KA, D Ozgediz, R Riviello, RY Hsia, S Jayaraman, SR Sullivan, and JG Meara. 2010. "Essential surgery: Integral to the right to health." *Health and Human Rights.* 12 (1): 137-52.

Mkandawire, Nyengo, Christopher Ngulube, and Christopher Lavy. 2008. "Orthopaedic Clinical Officer Program in Malawi: A Model for Providing Orthopaedic Care." *Clinical Orthopaedics and Related Research.* 466 (10): 2385-2391.

Nordberg E, I Mwobobia, and E Muniu. 2002. "Major and minor surgery output at district level in Kenya: review and issues in need of further research." *African Journal of Health Sciences.* 9 (1-2).

Ozgediz D, S Kijjambu, M Galukande, G Dubowitz, J Mabweijano, C Mijumbi, M Cherian, S Kaggwa, and S Luboga. 2008. "Africa's neglected surgical workforce crisis." *Lancet (London, England).* 371 (9613): 627-8.

Pollock, Jonathan D., Timothy P. Love, Bruce C. Steffes, David C. Thompson, John Mellinger, and Carl Haisch. 2011. "Is it Possible to Train Surgeons for Rural Africa? A Report of a Successful International Program." *World Journal of Surgery : Official Journal of the International Society of Surgery/Société Internationale De Chirurgie.* 35 (3): 493-499

Rosseel P, M Trelles, S Guilavogui, N Ford, and K Chu. 2010. "Ten years of experience training non-physician anesthesia providers in Haiti." *World Journal of Surgery.* 34 (3): 453-8.

Saswata B, F Omar, RJ Aubery, B Jaffer, and W Michael. 2005. "Bridging the health gap in Uganda: the surgical role of the clinical officer." *African Health Sciences.* 5 (1): 86-9.

Watters, D A, and Bayley, A C. 1987. *Training doctors and surgeons to meet the surgical needs of Africa.* http://www.ncbi.nlm.nih.gov/pmc/

articles/PMC1247780/.

Wilhelm TJ, IK Thawe, B Mwatibu, H Mothes, and S Post. 2011. "Efficacy of major general surgery performed by non-physician clinicians at a central hospital in Malawi." *Tropical Doctor.* 41 (2): 71-5.

Wilson, Amie, Lissauer, David, Thangaratinam, Shakila, Khan, Khalid S, MacArthur, Christine, and Coomarasamy, Arri. n.d. *A comparison of clinical officers with medical doctors on outcomes of caesarean section in the developing world: meta-analysis of controlled studies.* BMJ Publishing Group Ltd. http://www.pubmedcentral.nih.gov/articlerender.fcgi?artid=3272986.

Ystgaard B, and H Bolkan. 2013. "Surgery and task shifting in the rainforest." *Tidsskrift for Den Norske Lægeforening : Tidsskrift for Praktisk Medicin, Ny Række.* 133 (15): 1618-20.

PROFILES

DANIEL SAPAYIA

Superintendent, AIC Kajiado Child Care Center (KCCC)

Daniel Sapayia greets you with a big smile and a ready handshake. Outwardly, he has changed in the years since his photo was taken in the 1980s for the cover of Georgie Orme's book, *In Strength Not Our Own* (see previous footnote). Inwardly, his heart and generous spirit still overflow with enthusiasm for his work at KCCC.

A victim of polio himself, he walks with an uneven gait. When he is not wearing braces, which is most of the time, his knees seem to bend backwards a bit when he walks. But other than that, there is no way to know that he has experienced some of the same challenges encountered by the disabled that he serves.

I first visited Kajiado only a year after Daniel had arrived. We were all in a steep learning curve. He recalls, "I came to Kajiado in 1981 as a cobbler, a shoe-maker. Georgie and I knew nothing about managing disabled children. But the Lord is so good. He led us through the challenges."

In 1988, Dr. Kim, an orthopedic surgeon from Wilson Leprosy and Rehabilitation Hospital in South Korea, came to Kijabe for three weeks to help with the treatment of disabled children. He also came to teach me. We took him to Kajiado to evaluate the children there. Many from KCCC and other sites came for operations. During this time there were insufficient beds in the hospital for these added patients, so the chapel became a ward. Georgie provided nursing care during the day, and I slept in the chapel at night. The first call for night care went to some summer college student volunteers. If the needs were more complicated than they could handle, they would awaken me for help. Dr. Kim did about 60 operations during the time he was there.

Most of these patients needed the final touch – the appliances – that only Daniel could provide. These appliances included braces, special shoes, crutches, etc. It is the "et cetera" part that made Daniel's work so challenging. We were sometimes seeing children with needs that were not described in the normal books. We were also working under circumstances that were not common in the west, such as the terrain, the lack of financial assets, and the lack of equipment.

So Daniel first went to Nairobi to learn from orthopedic technicians who did that kind of work. He sat in on workshops and brought back sample calipers, trying with his limited equipment to copy them. "Sometimes it worked, sometimes it didn't," he admits. There was a time in the early work with the disabled at Kijabe when we had no orthopedic workshop and were totally dependent on Daniel to make braces for patients at Kijabe, Lamu and other locations.

Eventually Georgie sent Daniel to Kilimanjaro Medical Training Center in Tanzania (TATCOT) where he received a diploma in orthopedic technology. The training at Kilimanjaro involved the use of very sophisticated machines to produce prostheses and braces. Although he learned a lot, that machinery was not available at Kajiado.

When Dr. Kim invited Daniel and Georgie to visit Korea for additional training, they gratefully accepted. While Georgie studied management and assessment of the disabled,

Daniel trained in the orthopedic workshop. The technology at Wilson was simpler and easier and did not require the kind of equipment that was often used in Tanzania. It was far more applicable to a setting like Kajiado.

In 1996 Georgie went on home assignment for a year and appointed Daniel Acting Superintendent at KCCC. At the end of that year, Georgie, AIM, and the Africa Inland Church realized that the center was doing well without a "missionary presence." So Daniel was confirmed as the new Superintendent.

In many ways this was an answer to Georgie's hopes and prayers. Before retirement, Georgie started another small home, a branch of KCCC, in Baringo. Daniel continues to go there three times a year to assess children. He has also received additional training at Kikuyu Rehabilitation Hospital in the assessment of children with cerebral palsy.

Hundreds of children have passed through the center, and some still visit on an outpatient basis. Today, it not only serves children with polio, cerebral palsy, and tuberculosis, but also children with osteomyelitis, spina bifida, hydrocephalus, clubfeet, congenital limb deformity, etc. Due to the design of Maasai homes with an open fire in the center, many children also arrive with burns sustained by falling onto hot coals. If they are not treated immediately, infection can occur, often resulting in contractures that require more specialized care.[103]

The center can accommodate 80 children, but usually houses 60 – 65. They try to keep five beds available at all times for emergency or unexpected admissions. Twenty-one staff

103 Information in this paragraph was obtained from B. Watson's HealthServe report, Issue 6, June 2002.

members work there, including housemothers, teachers, nurses, physical therapists, orthopedic technologists, administrators, night guards, a cook, and a driver.

The center now has a small 4-bed maternity ward and a dispensary. All the nurses are trained in midwifery and a baby is delivered almost every other night. The gospel is preached daily and sometimes the local pastor comes in on clinic day to give a message.

Funding has always been an issue. Christoffel-Blinden Mission (CBM), Liliane Foundation, and AIM in both the UK and US donate regularly. Parents are asked to contribute what they can. But Daniel admits that sometimes the staff must wait a while, up to an entire month, to receive their wages. The staff continues working and trusting God to provide.

They know they are making a difference. "Disability is not inability," Daniel instructs. Some of the children who came through KCCC are now leaders in the community. One is a member of the Kenyan parliament; one is a member of the county assembly; one is the Minister of Finance for Kajiado County. Many others are teachers, accountants and secretaries. These are not traditional Maasai professions. Kajiado has been the place where many have had the opportunity to be educated to assume these jobs.

Daniel says confidently, "Jesus told us He would leave us with the Holy Spirit. That is my living testimony. Jesus, who used to touch and heal, is still doing the same through our hands. Jesus is still here with us. He lives with us and heals people every day."

Amen!

DR. MARK NEWTON

Pediatric Anesthesiologist, Kijabe Hospital

In 1994, Mark Newton was in Philadelphia for several days with other doctors and medical students, sharing the Gospel with those living in the inner city while doing health care evaluations and immunizations. In the evenings, Mark, others from their team, and some of the inner city youth would play basketball. During one of these games, he shared that he would like to use his anesthesia skills in a mission setting in Africa. Ian, one of the medical students, told him, "You should meet my roommate's dad."

The roommate was my son Rick. Ian had spent part of a summer in our home in Kenya and was familiar with our work with disabled children.

So Mark e-mailed me and told me he was a pediatric anesthesiologist, a specialty that is seldom available in Africa. I told him that we really could use a person with his skills. From that point on we corresponded every two or three months. In 1996, Mark and his family came to Kijabe for a visit. In 1997, they moved to Kijabe and have made it their home for the last 18 years.

Mark accompanied me on a few trips into South Sudan. On one occasion we were a part of a Safe Harbor[104] team. Mark remembered that trip particularly well. "We stayed in this little village with these Catholic nuns in this very remote place." The village was Tonj and it had once been a thriving town. However, by the time we arrived it had been decimated by war, starvation, and disease. The whole village seemed to be in the late stages of starvation. They had resorted to eating

104 www.safeharbor.us

the leaves from the trees. The people appeared like walking skeletons.

After the shock of the gaunt people there, my sharpest memory was of the group of nuns who cared for adults ravaged by leprosy. Medicine to help delay the physical damage of this disease had been rarely available for the previous two decades. There were no amenities. The leprosy patients were missing fingers, toes, and feet, but they quietly expressed their thankfulness. I examined patients and even performed a minor surgical procedure in a schoolroom.

That afternoon the team returned to Lokichoggio in Northern Kenya, dropping Mark, Joe Grant (an orthopedist), and me off at Lui in Southern Sudan. We spent the late afternoon and night learning about the work of Samaritan's Purse at Lui and its dreams for the future. At that time the medical work was being done in a school. The old hospital site was too dangerous to use because it was heavily mined with explosives.

The others had flown on to Loki to arrange the purchase and transportation of food to be flown to Tonj the next day. This was a desperate effort to save some lives. On their return, the plane stopped at Lui so that Joe, Mark and I could accompany them back to Tonj. The people were gathered into groups of ten to twenty, and we distributed as much grain as we could during a hectic few hours.

Mark recalls, "We were trying to figure out this massive feeding program for all these people who were dying. We distributed all this food to thousands of people at a time when relief organizations weren't going in because it was too dangerous. It was like out of a movie or something. People who are starving are willing to kill each other for food. Mothers were willing to do anything they could to get food for their children. But the men were the strongest with the biggest sticks and controlled everybody." Those men were taken aside and told that they couldn't keep beating the women. If they would leave the women alone, they would be given a little extra food.

In the late afternoon, the pilot came to us and said, with some urgency, that we had to leave. He had been watching the storm clouds south of us and was very concerned. We left the remaining food with the village elders and asked them to give it to the nuns at the leprosy colony.

As we took off, the clouds became even more ominous. The pilot skirted the edge of the storm, flying east while seeking to find a passage south to Loki. When he found no alternate route, he turned south, directly into the storm.

I had never before, or since, seen a pilot lock his steering wheel, but that's what he did. The ride was really bumpy, and Mark began "to lose his lunch." We ended up passing all of the infamous black bags to him, but he needed more. The only bags left were those containing our own food. A few of us finished the remaining food so we could give the additional empty bags to Mark.

When we came out of the storm, a "Low Fuel" light began to flash. It flashed for the next hour or more. I began searching the ground for suitable landing sites, but saw none. Finally, as the sun was beginning to set, we landed at Loki, probably with nothing left in the gas tank but fumes. It has been a truly stressful day.

Mark happily survived that rocky flight and continued his work and ministry. In 1998, he started the "Slow Program" in anesthesiology for nurses, training one or two at a time for 6

-12 months. After that he worked with the Kenya Ministry of Health to develop a more comprehensive program with a formal curriculum. To date, that program has trained over 90 nurse anesthetists who work in various locations in Kenya. He has also trained some from South Sudan, nearly the only anesthetists in all of South Sudan. "Kijabe is really the only place in East Africa that trains nurses to do anesthesia at this high level," he explains.

Recently, General Electric Foundation awarded a grant to Kijabe Hospital to establish a duplicate of this training program in Western Kenya, where there are, Mark explains, "six million people, no anesthesia [services], a lot of disabled children and mothers who are dying." Perhaps someday Kijabe Hospital will no longer be the only place that trains anesthetists and more professionals will be available to provide this vital service. As Mark says, the bottom line is, "If you want to do surgery, you have to have someone do the anesthesia."

Mark and his wife, Sue, have been tremendous medical and spiritual additions to Kijabe and much of East Africa. Praise God for their contributions and their soft, compassionate, visionary dispositions.

VERONICAH NJAMBI

BK Admin Officer

Veronica Njambi first came to Kijabe as a patient. She had been in a very bad traffic accident when she was 12 years old and had multiple fractures of her left leg and arm. She was brought to the hospital very early in the morning, and I was the first doctor to see her. She stayed in the pediatric ward for three months, although her full recovery took years. I followed up with her at the mobile clinic in Nakuru. She would often come early in the morning and then stay and translate for me for the rest of the day.

We maintained contact, and when she finished secondary school, I invited her to join us at BethanyKids in 2005. At first she did data work, then was made the full-time receptionist, and then became coordinator for the outpatient clinic. Veronica was committed to the work with disabled children, loyal, conscientious...and also fun.

At one point, I gave her a book that tested her interests, character, and career options. "It turned out that I am a [people] person," she says. We helped her attend computer college, and after that she went on to get her degree in Business Administration with a Human Resources concentration.

One of Veronicah's biggest responsibilities is coordinating the Pan-Africa Academy of Christian surgeons program. It's always a joy to her to see doctors come with their families from different parts of Africa for three years, settle, and adapt to Kenyan culture. After training, they return to their countries to take care of the disabled children there.

She also coordinates housing for other medical professionals and non-medical guests who come to work short-term or long-term, and ensuring that they have a good experience while in Kijabe. Although apartments have been built behind the hospital, occasionally the demand exceeds the supply. She says that the hardest thing about her job is turning away people who would like to come, only because she can't provide housing. This limits the number of professionals who can help at any given time. Hopefully, as the hospital grows, more housing will become available and this will no longer be a limiting factor.

AGNES JERUTO

Nursing Supervisor, BKKH

Agnes finished nursing school at Moi Hospital in Eldoret, but had very limited contact with the disabled. In her entire time of training, she only encountered two babies with spina bifida and three with hydrocephalus. The nurses were told that those babies weren't expected to live, that they should only provide minimal care and allow them to die.

One year after completing her training, she came to work at Bethany Crippled Children's Centre. She changed her perspective about the disabled when she came to Kijabe. "My heart just moved for the children," she confesses.

She exhibited a unique desire to improve the care for children with hydrocephalus and spina bifida. She was one of the first to help the children with spina bifida in bladder evaluation and clean intermittent catheterization (CIC). BCCC was the first to do CIC in central Africa. Agnes was invited to various countries to teach about this technique. She was an extremely valuable member of our team.

She has now finished her BSN in nursing. She continues to work at BethanyKids at Kijabe Hospital. The hospital trains nurses now and their training rotation includes eight weeks at BethanyKids, learning how to better care for the disabled. Agnes is the one who does the nursing students' orientation. To counteract the pervasive cultural indifference to the disabled, she emphasizes that it is a privilege to care for the children at BK. Her gentle teaching is helping to train a new generation of compassionate caregivers and improving the lives of countless disabled children.

Agnes was the only staff person who chose to make the transition from the Bethany Crippled Children's Center to BethanyKids at Kijabe Hospital. It was a difficult decision for her. No one knew how the work would function in its new setting at the hospital. She was unsure how the pursuit of "rehab nursing," a relatively new concept in healthcare in Africa, would affect her nursing career. She says a lot of prayer went into the decision, and she discussed it at length with Dr. Tim Mead, one of the orthopedists at CURE. He told her, "If this is God's work and God's plan for you, go for it!" Both she and BethanyKids are glad she did!

DR. JOSEPH THEURI

Medical Director, CURE International, Kijabe

Some might call Dr. Theuri "Mr. Clubfoot." He has been the pioneer and moving force behind establishing a program to care for children with clubfeet throughout much of Kenya.

Dr. Theuri came to Kijabe Hospital in 1996 as an intern. In 1997, following his internship, he began working as an apprentice with BCCC. Over a three-year period he was taught about the care of disabled children and gradually given more and more responsibility. Dr. Theuri was an excellent doctor and a quick learner. Early in our time together, while we were still at Kijabe Hospital, I was operating on a child with a clubfoot. I casually asked him to guess how many clubfoot repairs he would need to assist on before he was ready to do them. He quickly replied, "About 35!" This estimate is likely much higher than most young doctors would give. To me this indicated a conscientious doctor who wanted to learn to do this procedure well.

After working with BCCC for three years he went to Uganda to obtain a Master's degree in Orthopedic Surgery at Makerere University. He was there from 2000 – 2003. Upon his return to Kijabe, he continued to work with BCCC/CURE.

CURE, like BethanyKids, is not just a surgical center. CURE calls itself a 50/50 ministry: 50% medical and 50% spiritual. Dr. Theuri explains, "A hospital is supposed to be medical and people focus on that. But here the spiritual ministry takes as much significance as the medical. If you only treat someone medically, you've only treated them 50%. This doesn't have to be done only by the 'spiritual team.' Everyone takes part in that. It's the attitude we have as a hospital and as individuals. This is a person – not a case, not a procedure, not a process. We must be aware of all the facets of that person's life."

He remembers that initially some missionaries did all the work. But finally missionaries began empowering the local people and, he emphasized, "that has helped a lot. There was a time in Kijabe when you could think of a Kenyan as a nurse, but not as a doctor. The doctors were missionaries. Then Kenyans became doctors. But they couldn't be surgeons. Finally, after a while there was more training and some of us became surgeons."

He's also encouraged that Kenyans are taking greater ownership of medical facilities and outreach. Recently he visited a clubfoot clinic in Nakuru that had been struggling with administration and supply issues. They did their own advocacy through the local government hierarchy, got support and now have a self-sustainable ministry. The facility has enough plaster for casting, children are being treated without charge, and the clinic can exist without the financial support of CURE.

His greatest struggle is when patients have complications. "It's emotionally draining for everyone and a burden that you carry home. Fortunately they're not very common, but you remember them a very long time."

But he enjoys being at a children's hospital. "Children are much easier to take care of. They have a nice way of looking at things. It gives you a sense of fulfillment, that you are doing something significant."

DANIEL KIMEU

Mobile Clinic Coordinator, CURE Kenya

Daniel was a young man from the Akamba tribe who had developed deformities from polio when he was just a few years old. With a brace on his left leg, he is able to ambulate reasonably well. Daniel first attended school near Machakos, and later attended Joytown Secondary School for the Disabled. That is where I first met him. After graduation he felt that he would like to work with the disabled. He went to the headmistress of Joytown to request a letter of reference.

Shortly thereafter he became aware of a job working with the disabled at Kijabe Hospital. Was he interested? He sure was! In June 1993, he traveled to Kijabe to meet with me and learn about our evolving work with disabled children. At that time, I wanted to increase the number of mobile clinics and I needed help. Daniel took the job and started immediately. We were a team of two.

Traveling is often prohibitively expensive for poor families in Kenya. (The average Kenyan lives on less than $2 per day,

and many on less than $1 per day.) The scattered mobile
clinics allowed patients to receive pre-operative assessment
and advice, as well as consistent follow-up care. One by one
we established a presence in various locations around Kenya:
Kajiado, Nakuru, Thika (Joytown), Kisumu (Joyland), Eldoret,
Matumaini, Nyahururu, Mombasa, Embu, Kitale and others.

Daniel began working for me at Kijabe Hospital in 1993. In
1998, he made the transition to Bethany Crippled Children's
Centre, where he helped in the Outpatient Department and
on mobile clinics. He also began taking classes to help him
improve his work skills, receiving a diploma in Public Relations
and Computer Studies. Daniel was a real "people person" and
knew the locations, diagnoses, and needs of hundreds of our
disabled children scattered around Kenya.

Daniel was always sensitive to the increased difficulty
in establishing the work in some areas. "Machakos is more
difficult than others," he explains. "There is a lot of stigma there
toward the disabled, and it's difficult to get [families of the
disabled] to come and learn." Our approach was to start with
the simple cases that brought great results, low complications,
and gave people confidence in the ministry. Those successes
eventually encouraged others in the community to bring more
of their disabled children for treatment.

Daniel offers a surprising observation. "We have a lot of
Muslims coming to clinics now with their disabled children.
The good thing [about them] is that if they know a place where
they can get help, they are good at spreading the information.
They will go back and seek out others who need help. They like
the Christian organization better than the government. They
feel more accepted and [know] they will get better services."

He's encouraged by the growth at BethanyKids at Kijabe

Hospital and CURE at Kijabe. He says that Kijabe Hospital, BK, and CURE operate somewhat like a polyclinic. "We live as brothers in a community. We are here for one purpose: to serve God in what we are doing. This is a work of God!"

DAVID KIMANI

"Physical therapist" and Brace-maker, BK (former)

In 1987, Roger Mailleffer, an RVA graduate, was in college preparing to become a physical therapist. He wrote asking if he could spend his summer vacation working in the Physical Therapy Department at Kijabe Hospital. I confessed to him that we had a small room and some equipment, but we had no therapist for him to work with at that time. He chose to come anyway and utilize his limited skills.

About two weeks after his arrival, he approached me with a suggestion. If we could give him someone to train, we would have a person who could help us when he left at the end of the summer. I suggested a few possible candidates. David Kimani, a former patient with polio who now wore a brace, seemed like the best candidate.

At the end of the summer when Roger left, David continued with the work. He helped with casts, postoperative care, and ultimately the fitting of many braces. At that time, we were operating on a large number of patients with the secondary effects of polio. Our braces were still being made at Kajiado.

In 1988, my family returned to the U.S. for a one-year furlough/home assignment. That year a donor offered to pay for David's training in orthopedic technology at Kilimanjaro Medical Training Centre in Tanzania. He attended and learned how to make braces, which turned out to be our first step in establishing a brace shop at Kijabe. In 1990, David traveled to Wilson Rehabilitation Hospital in South Korea to further his training.

David accompanied me on the early trips to Joytown and Nakuru and other mobile clinics, helping to bring children back to Kijabe for surgical care. Initially he was our "go-to" guy for therapy and later for all kinds of prosthetics. There's no underestimating David's value in the rehab effort at Kijabe Hospital during those early years. Many, many children in Kenya were able to walk as a result of David's expertise.

FRANCIS MBATHA

Communications Specialist, BK (former)

In April 2009, we added Francis Mbatha to the BK team. Francis had a diploma in TV Production from the Kenya Institute of Mass Communication. He was given the task of journaling the stories of patients and their families to put on the BK website. He also chronicled the work of our personnel and visitors. He developed great insight into the unique struggles and triumphs of the disabled and those who work with them.

Francis also began to produce DVDs for our outreach. These served three purposes: promotional, motivational, and educational. We made these available at the hospital, at mobile clinics, and in churches and other community organizations to inform the public of our services to the disabled and our ongoing needs.

Francis likes to tell a humorous story about how he learned a little lesson in the O.R. I was the surgeon during his second video shoot in the operating room. He had been previously warned that he shouldn't get physically close to patients during surgery. The ultimate intention of this precaution was to maintain sterility. Francis admits that one day that slipped his mind. He was "so enthralled and [involved in] shooting this encephalocele.[105] It was so amazing." In his excitement he almost touched the sterile sheets on the operating table.

At that point I shouted at him, "Francis! What are you doing there? That patient lying there is more important than any one of us in this room!" Francis was terrified. "I was lost!" he thought, "I wouldn't have my job anymore! I was shaking. My camera was shaking." Fortunately he had not compromised the sterile field and really was in no danger of losing his job. From that point on however, he filmed surgery at a healthy (pun intended) distance.

But the story illustrates an important philosophy at BK – the patient is the most important person in the operating room. Francis says BK is the "place that made my life turn around. I saw miracles happen each and every day."

DAVID NG'ANG'A

Bethany Kids Administrator, Kenya

Joytown Special School

For David, working with the disabled is somewhat of a family affair. He is Chaplain Mercy's[106] son.

In 2005, after the patients with hydrocephalus and spina bifida had transitioned back into Kijabe Hospital from BCCC, we needed a financial study to point out the benefits

105 An encephalocele is a neural tube defect characterized by sac-like protrusions of the brain and the membranes that cover it through openings in the skull. These defects are caused by failure of the neural tube to close completely during fetal development.
106 See profile.

Kijabe Hospital could expect by having BethanyKids housed at their institution. The study involved gathering patient records, determining revenue and costs, inputting that data into a customized data base, and then analyzing the results to determine BK's impact on the hospital's budget.

David had recently graduated from Daystar University with a double major in Business Management and Management and Accounting. We reviewed his CV and hired him on a limited contract basis. It was his first professional job. David continued his job hunt, even while doing this study for BK. That was understandable, and we agreed to proceed until a better and more permanent position became available for him.

David describes the job as "tedious." All the money that changed hands had to be tracked and categorized. After a month, he had enough information to develop a comprehensive report. As it turned out, BK was providing 30% of KH's surgical revenue, a significant contribution. We had him present the report to the hospital leadership, an assignment that made him really nervous. "I didn't want to do it," he admits. But he did a fine job.

David's contract for that study ended, but at the end of August 2005, I called him again. I was the BK medical director and wanted him to be my administrative assistant. I explained that his role would be different from Oscar Ogwang's, and I felt that we could really use both of them.

By early 2006, he had been promoted to "Executive Administrative Assistant" and, in addition to his many other duties, was taking trips with me to Dadaab and Kakuma Refugee Camps. He was a fast learner. When the organizational structure of BRRI changed, he helped me with BK-Africa and took exploratory trips to Tanzania and Madagascar.

When Joytown Special School entered into its Memorandum of Understanding with BethanyKids in September 2009, David, as BK-Africa Administrator, became BethanyKids' Administrator for Kenya, located at Joytown. BK provides and oversees the rehabilitation services at the school and assists with some other special projects, such as improvements to the bathrooms and guesthouse and the development of the central laundry. Doctors from CURE and BK visit once each term and twice in January to identify any new medical/surgical needs.

There are many ways in which Millie and I see David somewhat like a son. Joshua and Philip treat him a lot like a brother, and they very much enjoy their time with him. In my opinion, having David working with BethanyKids has been wonderful. David's greatest joy in his work at Joytown is seeing the kids everyday. He commented, "Even when I'm having a terrible day, when I come here I know I will end up happy."

JULIANA AUMA

Spina Bifida and Hydrocephalus Association of Kenya (SHAK)[107]

International Federation for Spina Bifida and Hydrocephalus (IF)

House of Hope Guesthouse, Kijabe

Juliana became pregnant with Phoebe while she was still in high school. When her daughter was born with spina bifida and hydrocephalus, the staff told her, "Her head is full of water and she doesn't have a brain. She will die." She was advised to leave Phoebe in the hospital because she would never enjoy taking care of her. "Those were cruel words," Juliana recalls.

107 http://www.bethanykids.org/our-work/shak

She was falsely accused of causing her daughter's condition. "In Africa, if you have a child with a disability, it is bad. They blame you," she reports sadly. She ignored the accusations and took Phoebe home. A neighbor who was a medical student at the University of Nairobi examined Phoebe and suggested that Juliana take her to Kenyatta Hospital. For three months Juliana took Phoebe into the hospital every morning and came home every night without ever seeing a physician. She was always told to "come back tomorrow." Finally someone told Juliana it would be two years before they could operate on her daughter. The waiting list was just too long.

She felt defeated. When a neighbor realized that she wasn't going to the hospital anymore, she urged Juliana to take her story to the newspapers. If they printed it, maybe someone would help.

So Juliana did. Her story was reported in The Standard, complete with a photo. "Three days later we were in a very expensive hospital, Gertrude Gardens' Children's Hospital, in Nairobi." The management at the hospital read her story and thought Juliana was very brave. They took Phoebe as a charity case. Juliana didn't pay a single penny for her care.

They decreased the pressure in Phoebe's brain by inserting a shunt. They also closed the defect on her back. However, by age three she still couldn't stand up or control her bowel or bladder. When she was four, Juliana took her to one of BCCC's mobile clinics at the headquarters of the Association for Disabled People in Kenya (APDK) in Nairobi. That was where I first met her.

I suggested that they come to Kijabe so that Phoebe could be fitted for braces. Juliana arrived with so many questions. We answered them as best we could. When Juliana returned to Nairobi, she refused keep this newfound knowledge to herself. She returned to Kenyatta Hospital, contacted parents of children with SB and HC, and formed a support group.

Now there are 12 support groups in Kenya, registered nationally under the umbrella of the Spina Bifida and Hydrocephalus Association of Kenya (SHAK). SHAK parents go to clinics with BK staff to recruit new support group members and invite them to educational workshops done by BK nurses. SHAK offers encouragement and helps parents to understand what to expect. "Nobody told me it would take [so] long for Phoebe's bladder to be trained," Juliana says. She had to do CIC for Phoebe every three hours for three or four years. "Many parents think that as soon as the child is trained in CIC that the bladder will be immediately controlled and the child won't leak anymore. [When that doesn't happen] they wonder why it's 'not working' when they are doing everything right." SHAK members are there to reassure them that bladder training takes time and encourage them to persevere.

In 2012 the International Foundation for Spina Bifida and Hydrocephalus (IF) president, Pierre Mertens, visited Kijabe to help SHAK start the Spina Bifida and Hydrocephalus Interdisciplinary Program (SHIP). In the SHIP program, parents of the disabled are provided with a small booklet that they take with their child to every setting: clinic, school, and therapy. Entries about the child's development are added at each location. It's a holistic approach to their care that provides a way for parents and professionals to consistently track and communicate each child's progress and needs.

Pierre Mertens had lunch with Juliana, her parents, and some youth with SB during that visit. They discussed the idea for a guesthouse for the families of the disabled who were receiving care at BethanyKids. In 2013, it became a reality. IF established a safe, comfortable home, called House of Hope, where families of the disabled can stay while their children receive rehab services at BethanyKids. It's fully funded by IF Childhelp, including rent, utility bills, food, and allowances for Juliana (who lives there and runs the facility) and Phyllis Migasha, the chairperson of the Nairobi support group. Parents are referred to the guesthouse through BK.

The house, perched on a ledge overlooking a narrow, forested valley, has several large bedrooms furnished with wide bunk beds. This allows mothers to have their children beside them at night, and enjoy the company of other moms. A nice kitchen is available for meal preparation, and Juliana tends a thriving vegetable garden and keeps several chickens to provide fresh eggs.

Juliana expects that the support groups and the work at the guesthouse will continue to grow. "Our voices have begun to make a change in our society," she says with a smile.

WILLIS OBUNGA

Development and Communications Coordinator, BK

Willis has a deep rich voice and a smile that lights up a room. Both characteristics are in overdrive when he tells others about working with disabled children. But he admits that wasn't always the case. "The first time I saw a child with a huge head, I ran away!"

I first met Willis while I was still at Bethany Crippled Children's Centre. His fiancée Janet was in nurses' training at Kijabe and introduced us. He had a diploma in Bible and

Theology from Moffatt Bible College and was a pastor in Kericho, a town in western Kenya.

Willis would occasionally come and stay with us while visiting Janet in Kijabe. As their wedding date approached, they asked Millie and me if we would do some marriage counseling with them. We agreed, and eventually attended their wedding in Kericho.

By the time of their wedding, Janet had graduated from nursing school and was working at a local hospital near Kericho. During their month-long holiday, she and Willis came to Kijabe where she volunteered at Bethany Crippled Children's Centre. Because we needed nurses, we offered her a job.

To me, she and Willis were a "package deal." I felt that we needed better public relations, so Willis came to work under my direction. His first priorities were learning how to take photographs, record videos, and use the computer. He literally began at "square one," playing with the cameras and studying photos taken by professional photographers in books that I loaned to him. He easily mastered both the camera work and the computer. Eventually he earned a bachelor's degree by extension at Kenya Methodist University, and went on to earn a master's degree in Communications at Daystar University in 2010.

With the help of others, he initiated our video program. He videotapes and records patient stories, develops articles for the BK website and Facebook pages, and helps secure funding for patient surgeries. Each month he sends about 16 – 17 patient profiles to the crowd-funding site WATSI[108], which has been very helpful in providing assistance for many of our disabled

---

108 https://watsi.org/

children. Initially, over 90% of the patient profiles submitted received some funding. In 2014, BK patients secured almost 10 million Ksh (approx. 10,000 USD) through this organization.

Community education initiatives are also a part of Willis' job description. Over the last few years BK has produced short radio features to inform women of childbearing age about the importance of taking folic acid supplements before pregnancy to help prevent spina bifida. They were recorded in several different tribal dialects to reach isolated populations with limited access to medical information. Another avenue has been through visits to local churches. His goal is to sensitize them to the plight of disabled children, encourage them to reach out to families of the disabled in their communities, and solicit congregational support. It's a huge task. But with his warm voice and bright smile, Willis is just the man for the job.

JUSTUS MARETE

BethanyKids Director for Africa (Administrative Services)

The BethanyKids Africa staff reports to the Director for Africa, Justus Marete. Justus was the executive director at Kijabe Hospital when the BCCC patients made their famous crossing to Kijabe Hospital in 2004. He remembers many early morning meetings with chai that went into hammering out the agreement between the hospital and BK. "More than 20 meetings!" he says, with a chuckle.

In 2011, after eight years of overseeing positive growth at Kijabe Hospital, he applied to become the director of BethanyKids, Africa. The ministry to the disabled at both BCCC and BK was part of what attracted Justus. Previously BCCC had helped his own daughter with a physical disability.

Many organizations now partner with BethanyKids and have helped expand the work in Kenya. These include the Christian Health Association of Kenya (CHAK)[109], the International Federation of Spina Bifida and Hydrocephalus (IFSBH), the Spina Bifida and Hydrocephalus Association of Kenya[110], Samaritan's Purse, WATSI, and AIM, to name a few. He says there are now over 40 hospitals and 500 lower lever health facilities who are part of the CHAK network.

BK assists selected staff members to continue their education and enhance their on-the-job skills. Special training in pediatric nursing, pediatric surgery, and pediatric neurosurgery were introduced during the last few years. Some are in association with the College of Surgeons of Eastern, Central, and Southern Africa (COSECSA) and the PanAfrican Academy of Christian Surgeons (PAACS). As of this printing, the following physicians have completed or will complete their training through BKKH:

> 1. Dr. Heuric Rakotomalala was the first to complete pediatric surgery training and is now serving in Southern Madagascar.

> 2. Dr. Catherine Mung'ong'o trained in pediatric surgery and is now serving in Northern Tanzania.

> 3. Dr. Frehun Ayele completed pediatric surgery training and is now serving in Ethiopia.

> 4. Dr. Martin Situma completed pediatric surgery training and is now serving in South Western Uganda at Mbarara University Hospital.

---

109 http://www.chak.or.ke/fin/
110 See profile page for Juliana Auma.

5. Dr. Aiah Lebbie completed pediatric surgery training and is now serving in Sierra Leone.

6. Dr. Humphrey Okechi completed pediatric neurosurgery training and is now serving with BethanKids at Kijabe.

7. Dr. Addisalem completed pediatric neurosurgery surgery in August 2015 and will be returning to Ethiopia.

8. Drs. Naomi & Dan Ochieng are in their second year of neurosurgical training in South Africa. They have agreed to work at Kijabe Hospital in association with BK following their training.

9. Dr Edmund Ntaganda is scheduled to complete his pediatric surgery training in 2016 and will serve in Rwanda, his home country.

10. Dr. George Ngock is in his first year of training in pediatric surgery and will serve in Cameroon when he qualifies.

11. Dr. Grace Muthoni is training in neurosurgery and is matriculated at the University of Nairobi.

12. Dr. Ken Muma completed training in pediatric surgery and is now serving at Kijabe Hospital.

Through these training programs at BethanyKids at Kijabe Hospital, highly qualified specialists will finally be available in parts of Africa where they are needed. These 13 doctors can have a dramatic impact if each shares his or her expertise to train others. That's an exciting prospect for the future care of the disabled.

TRACEY HAGMAN

Heshima Children's Center[111]

It's a long, dusty road to get to Heshima, past Lenana School, through Ngando slum. You begin to wonder if you've taken a wrong turn and are going to end up in the bush somewhere. But finally the Heshima sign appears, pointing to a very tall cinder-block wall and a huge gate. You have arrived.

Tracey and Eric Hagman founded Heshima Children's Center in 2010, and it is a true oasis for disabled children and their mothers. When the gates open, it's like you've stepped into another world. The gardens are full of bright blooming flowers, the walkways are smooth and swept, and the air is full of soft voices and gentle laughter.

Tracey first came to Kenya with AIM in 1989 and worked at RVA. She returned to the U.S., met and married Eric. They had two children: Sam, now a medical student in the States, and Simon, now 19. Simon was born at only 22 weeks gestation and weighed only 1 lb. After two years in the hospital, three heart attacks, and other complications, Simon finally came home. Although he still has significant learning disabilities and wears glasses, "he's the healthiest one in the family!" Tracey laughs.

The Hagmans were successful in the states. Eric had his own thriving construction company. They were very involved with a church. But eventually God put it on their hearts to return to Africa and go into mission work. They explored options and Eric was offered the Nairobi-based job as African director of Wycliffe Associates.

"People didn't understand [why we were leaving the U.S.],"

---

111 http://www.heshimachildrenscenter.org/

Tracey says. "We had a handicapped son. How was that going to work in a third-world country?"

Eric and Tracey knew that Simon would need special education and therapy. They found some European therapists in Kenya who agreed to work with him. Then when Simon was going into first grade, they approached West Nairobi School – an international school with an American curriculum – to consider a special education program. After many e-mails and lots of prayer, a special education teacher agreed to come over for two years and start the program.

In 2006 or 2007, Tracey decided to start her own ministry to Kenyan special needs children. She and a Kenyan teacher rented a room in Ngando slum, raised funds, and started taking care of disabled kids. Eventually it outgrew the single room, so they rented a second apartment and broke down the wall between the two to enlarge the space. As Tracey raised money, they rented more space, hired more people, and enrolled more kids. By 2010, Tracey's little makeshift childcare center was serving eight children and employed five staff. But, she says, "The place was getting worse and worse. No electricity, no running water, rats, and an outhouse that was shared by the public." She felt oppression and heaviness there. "Satan is dirty and low and keeps you down. God is light and clean and organized," she says.

So, in 2010, she and Eric decided to purchase land for a larger, nicer facility. "Buying land in Kenya is very complicated. It was a long process," she reports. But they knew God was directing their efforts and finally settled on the property they now own. Eric started another construction company, Dignity Development, to provide jobs for local Kenyans, build their complex, and also handle building projects for other NGOs.

They raised money for each Heshima construction project as they went along. First they built the wall, then the water building for Maji Kwa Heshima ("Water for Dignity"), where locals can purchase fresh clean water for a nominal amount. The children's center moved into a large multi-purpose building in 2012 when they had about a dozen children enrolled. Their main building still isn't built yet. The plans call for it to be L-shaped with 2-stories, housing therapy rooms, and spaces for other educational options.

All the administrators, managers, and therapists at Heshima are Kenyan and, at this writing, the Hagmans employ over 50 people. The mothers of the enrolled children help pay their children's school fees by working as helpers, cooks, aides, and – in a stroke of genius – as artisans in the Dignity Designs shop.

Tracey taught some of the women how to make beautiful jewelry, scarves, and other items that she sells at an on-site gift shop and through Fair Trade[112] outlets and jewelry parties hosted by private supporters in the states. Everything is designed for the Western market and made with indigenous trade beads, cow bone, recycled brass, and other African materials.

Heshima is a shining example of a sustainable model to assist disabled children and their families in Africa. And "it all came from Simon!" Tracey laughs.

---

112 http://fairtradeusa.org/

Addendum

So you think you might like to work abroad?

The word missionary is defined as "a sent one." All Christians have been sent by God to represent Him in this world, spreading the good news of the Gospel wherever we find ourselves. Be careful of the word "all" – it may dilute your sense of individual, personal responsibility. I believe that the Scriptures teach that we will ALL individually stand before the Lord and give an explanation of how we have used the gifts and talents that He has given us. I believe that He expects something unique out of each of us, and this uniqueness is meant to have His chosen impact upon the world.

You may not be a doctor, a nurse, a therapist, a pastor, or even an adult. But some of you reading right now might feel the tug to go as God's ambassador to a foreign setting for an extended period of time. The Joytown motto is instructive:

> "I am only one, but I am one. I cannot do everything, but I can do something. What I can do I ought to do. And what I ought to do, by the grace of God, I will do."

Where do you start? How do you prepare? Most sending organizations have excellent orientation and training programs, but the best advice usually comes from those who live and work in the field. We asked Kenyan nationals, plus our friends and colleagues on the field, what they would like to tell someone interested in a missionary career in Africa, or for that matter, any developing country. We received a wide variety of insightful and practical suggestions.

Mike Delorenzo was an AIM Air pilot for 12 years and has helped with AIM's media ministry for the last five. He and his wife Renee went to Africa right after they were married. They "never had an adult life in America. Never owned a house." He laughs that they were "pretty green in every way!"

When he speaks to young people, he uses what he calls his "Matthew 11, Matthew 28 speech." He explains that in the first passage, Jesus calls us to "come to him" and in the second passage he tells us to "go and make disciples." He says we have to continually come to Jesus in order to continually go. So the first requirement is to develop a healthy spiritual life and relationship with Jesus.

Mike reports that their missionary orientation stressed the need for trust, flexibility, and teachability on the field. Those are important and necessary. But nobody mentioned two things he also thinks are essential: wisdom and courage. One must be willing to take risks. "You will be afraid, stretched, and uncomfortable," he says. Western culture epitomizes comfort and security. "Here we're in an atmosphere of control, safety, and limited risk. Avoiding risk. God calls us to a life of risk. God is sovereign. There are no guaranteed outcomes."

Long-time friend Scott Taylor, former Air Force fighter pilot and member of the BethanyKids board, agrees. "Strip off the 'insulation' of the desire for comfort and safety and keeping the world's needs at arm's length. Overcome fear with faith. The gift of being born in America qualifies and equips you to do anything God wants you to do." I would add that it would ultimately be through the power of the Holy Spirit.

Going hand-in-hand with that is wisdom and that includes developing a good understanding of the culture where you feel lead to serve. Veronicah Njambi says that if you are considering Africa, "Get to know how Africans are. Learn to value other people. Be prepared. There are shortages of facilities, equipment. There will be unexpected challenges."

Agnes Jeruto adds that a newcomer should value nationals and those who have been there longer, especially in a medical setting where many staffing levels work together. "Someone may have a lower education than you do, but has been in the field a long time. A new person coming in may have the theory, but not the practical [experience]," she says. Because she is a nursing supervisor, she is particularly sensitive to this issue where nurses are concerned. "Respect the nurses, listen to them. The patients spend most of their time with the nurses, especially the night nurses. They have been with the patients without doctor input all night." And, last but not least, "Listen to what the patient tells you!"

Although the wise counsel of others is important in making a decision to work overseas, Daniel Sapayia cautions, "Not everybody will be happy about what you are doing. Maybe your own people in the church won't understand." But, he adds, "If God is calling you, don't hesitate. You will be rewarded in a very special way."

David Ng'ang'a at Joytown emphasizes, "The need is huge. We need people to train, to walk with us, [to help us] improve our rehab approach. We need many different services, such as aqua therapy, speech therapy, surgery. Just come and help! We'll find a place for you!"

Kijabe Hospital surgeon Dr. Peter Bird advises medical students to "be as broad as you can in your training" while acknowledging that "that can be hard to do." His medical college in Australia has what is called a "rural stream" where students get more training in basic surgical procedures and other medical specialties. This would be a good foundation for someone interested in practicing medicine in the developing world.

Dr. Erik Hansen has advice for prioritizing the many needs and projects in your country of service. "Be ready to say 'no.' The needs are great. I talked to a long-term missionary who said that when she first got on the field in Nigeria, she said 'no' to everything but a cup of coffee." He's heard this echoed over and over again by experienced missionaries. "It's exciting and we feel a calling, a sense of arrival. Excited to get going and be a part of it. People are going to ask you to do anything and everything. If you try to do everything, you'll burn out and fail. It's a lot easier to take back a 'no' than take back a 'yes.'" He adds, "Be wise about your family. Have a margin. Every 'yes' is a 'no' to something else. Often that 'no' is your kids or spouse." He adds that he told his mission board, "I want to be a great husband, a great father, and a great surgeon – in that order!" He admits that his wife and kids would say he falls short, but that's his heart and it's a good example for all of us.

It goes without saying that you and your spouse should be in total agreement about your field assignment, and that you work well as a team. Many people have commented that Millie is as much a part of the work with the disabled behind the scenes as I have been on the scenes. The truth is that I could not have accomplished any of it without her support and encouragement. I was away for long periods of time in dangerous areas, and at the hospital from the early morning hours until late at night. She always kept the home fires burning and stayed constant in prayer for my return. She never complained (except for that brief episode with the diapers in the Islands that would have exasperated anyone!) We had people come to our home for dinner on short notice and she always welcomed them with a smile and a hug. Some houseguests stayed with us for months at a time. She became an integral part of the community, teaching at RVA, hosting Bible study groups and prayer meetings, helping with Bible clubs at national schools – to name just a few of the many hats she wore.

Now, if this sounds like someone who was too good to be true, let me insert this insightful comment from Mike Delorenzo's wife Renee: "Millie chose joy." Were there moments of anxiety and concern? Of course! Sometimes it wasn't easy, but she chose joy as her life song and the background music for our marriage and family life. She never allowed frustration to become her own disability.

Some candidates for overseas work have concerns about their children. Third-culture kids (TCK's) or "missionary kids" (MKs) are a special breed. Their experiences are unlike those of their peers in either their countries of origin or their countries of service. As a result, they often don't feel totally at home in either place.

Dr. Tim Mead, an orthopedic surgeon who worked at BCCC in Kenya for 12 years and who now serves as medical director for CURE International, tells an interesting story that illustrates this. "When my son went to college, he was asked about the 'most fun' thing he had ever done. Some kids talked about going to Disney [World], some went overseas [on vacations], and some went camping up north. Aaron said, 'I think it's when I go with my friends and we camp in the valley and bring our pikis (old motorcycles). We get up in the morning and chase zebras and gazelles with them." The lady in charge told Aaron that it was supposed to be something they really did, not something they dream about doing. And Aaron told her 'I have done that!'"

Although that story is humorous, it has a serious edge. Your kids will not always "fit in." But, Dr. Mead adds, "Your children will benefit from living overseas. It improves their worldview and helps them see the true priorities in life. Money doesn't bring you lasting joy."

Fred Muiriri, former IT specialist at BK, echoes that theme. He suggests that missionaries "have a calling not based on prestige or fame or money." Although prestige and fame can be set aside, unfortunately the need for money is still very much a part of our fallen world. Dr. Mead suggests trying to "be as debt-free as possible" when you go on the field. Those destined for work abroad need to begin early to minimize their debts. This may not be very realistic in this day and age with college costs rising almost daily. Most healthcare workers have school debt when they graduate and paying off those loans can take decades. One organization called MedSend[113] is trying to help. This organization assists healthcare professionals serve on the field by making their monthly educational loan payments while they are on assignment overseas.

This addendum is just a small sample of good advice from seasoned missionaries. Many, many books have been written to guide those who feel called to overseas careers. Most can be easily obtained through Amazon.com. Here are a few titles that were helpful to Millie and me throughout our career:

Anderson, Courtney. 1956. *To the Golden Shore: the Life of Adoniram Judson.* Boston: Little, Brown.

Gorforth, Mrs. Rosalind Bellsmith. 1937. *Goforth of China.* Grand

113 http://www.medsend.org/

Rapids, Mich: Zondervan Pub. House.

Grubb, Norman P. 1952. *Rees Howells: Intercessor.* Fort Washington, Pa: Christian Literature Crusade.

Elliot, Elisabeth. 1987. *A Chance to Die: The life and legacy of Amy Carmichael.* Old Tappan, N.J.: F.H. Revell Co.

Francis, Mabel, and Gerald B. Smith. 1968. *One Shall Chase a Thousand.* Harrisburg, Pa: Christian Publications.

Rockness, Miriam Huffman. 2003. *A Passion for the Impossible: The life of Lilias Trotter.* Grand Rapids, MI: Discovery House Publishers.

McClung, Floyd. 1988. *Living on the Devil's Doorstep: The McClung family story.* Waco, Tex: Word Books.

Wilson, Dorothy Clarke. 1989. *Ten Fingers for God: The life and work of Paul Brand.* Grand Rapids, Mich: Zondervan Pub. House.

Zacharias, Ravi K., and Scott Sawyer. 2006. *Walking from East to West: God in the Shadows.* Grand Rapids, Mich: Zondervan.

Elliot, Elisabeth. 1958. *Shadow of the Almighty: The life & testament of Jim Elliot.* New York: Harper.

Hamlin, Catherine, and John Little. 2004. *The Hospital by the River: A story of hope.* Oxford, UK: Monarch Books.

Boyd, Andrew. 1998. *Baroness Cox: a Voice for the Voiceless.* [Oxford, England]: Lion.

Lewis, Gregg. 2007. *Miracle at Tenwek: the life of Dr. Ernie Steury.* Grand Rapids, MI: Discovery House Publishers.

Ripken, Nik, and Gregg Lewis. 2013. *The Insanity of God: a True Story of Faith Resurrecte*d. Nashville, Tenn: B&H Publishing Group.

Howard, David M. 2012. *What I saw God Do: Reflections on a lifetime in missio*ns. United States: CreateSpace.

Hirsi Ali, Ayaan. 2007. *Infidel.* New York: Free Press.

Hirsi Ali, Ayaan. 2010. *Nomad.* Toronto: A.A. Knopf Canada.

Platt, David. 2010. *Radical: Taking back your faith from the American Dream.* Colorado Springs, Colo: Multnomah Books.

Piper, John. 2003. *Don't Waste Your Life.* Wheaton, Ill: Crossway Books.

Foulkes, James, and Joe Lacy. 2005. *To Africa With Love: A Bush Doc's Story.* Franklin, Tn: Providence House Publishers.

Roseveare, Helen. 1966. *Give Me This Mountain; An Autobiography.* Grand Rapids: Eerdmans.

Swift, Catherine M. 1990. *Eric Liddell.* Minneapolis, Minn: Bethany House Publishers.

Doyle, Tom, and Greg Webster. 2012. *Dreams and Visions: Is Jesus Awakening the Muslim World?* Nashville, Tenn: Thomas Nelson.

FINAL ACKNOWLEDGMENTS
from Diane Coleman

First and foremost, I'd like to thank Linda Swanson for introducing me by e-mail to Dr. Bransford and recommending me for this wonderful project. Thank you, Dr. Bransford, for sharing your heart for the disabled and giving me the privilege of assisting you to make your work and dream known to a larger audience. To God, indeed, be the glory!

Another big thank you goes to Thrive Ministries[114] for allowing me to serve on its retreat team in Tanzania in the fall of 2014. This enabled me to continue on to Kenya to visit BethanyKids at Kijabe Hospital, interview Dr. Bransford's many colleagues and patients, and deepen my understanding of his amazing work with the disabled.

Generous friends and family who helped fund that trip include the following: The DeGol Family Foundation, Jay and Georgann French, Bill and Georgina Hitz, Dwayne and Deborah Kepner, Ann Rasmus, Mike and Cindy Ryan, Tom and Denise Seymour, Hank and Jenny Snyder, Dan and Michele Staley, Bruce and Kathleen Yager, Susan Coleman, Ann Coleman, Lynn Garcia, Tom Kaiser, Don and Lori Lewis, Dr. Richard and Leslie Rayner, Marlin and Elaine Scheidler, Kyle and Allison Shank, Bill and Sharon Sones, John and Mary Stansfield, Dr. Anees and Fareda Zaka, Lorne and Jane Patrick, Sharon Reinhart, Bobby and Linda Scott, Graham and Carla Snyder, Dennis and Yvonne Souder, Dan and Deb Stuber, and Dr. Jim and Bev Barnett. A special thanks goes to the Barnetts, who hosted me for three days while I recorded

---

114 https://www.thriveministry.org/

Dr. Bill Barnett's wonderful memories. I am also very grateful to Lorne and Jane Patrick, who allowed me to use their quiet and comfortable lake house as a writing retreat. What a great place to write!

I was also deeply blessed by the constant prayer support of my church, Freedom Bible Fellowship in Dauphin, PA, and pastor, Mark Barninger.

My sincere appreciation also goes to the following people who were so helpful to me in Kenya: the Marete family in Kijabe for hosting me for dinner three nights (even bringing dinner to me at the motel on the one night I couldn't be with them!); the Mitchell family at RVA (Bruce, Susan, and Sammy) for allowing me – a stranger! – to stay in their spare room; John Githii for providing great reliable transportation to Kijabe, Thika, and Kajiado; and the kind staff at AIM Mayfield guesthouse in Nairobi for their good care. A big thankyou goes to all the interviewees who took time out of their busy schedules to talk to me. Some traveled for hours over great distances to tell me their stories because they have such admiration and respect for Dr. Bransford and all he has done for them. I'd also like to thank Patty Arensen for suggesting that I visit Heshima Children's Center and Tracey Hagman for welcoming me on such short notice.

Another person who deserves our appreciation is Kelsey McFaul, a graduate student at Stanford University, who graciously conducted preliminary interviews of staff at Kijabe Hospital a few months before my arrival there. The information she provided enabled me to fine-tune many of my followup interviews and maximize my time in Kijabe.

I'd like to thank Millie Bransford, who provided cheerful hospitality, insight, editing suggestions, and constant encouragement to Dick and me as we labored over many drafts and versions. Also, we deeply appreciate the work of Cindy Blomquist, Nat Belz, and Mike Delorenzo, our editors, who groomed the manuscript to prepare it for publication. Their expertise was invaluable in bringing this book to print.

Last, but not least, thank you to my daughter Juliana Schutte for assisting me with transcribing interviews (a BIG job!) and to my dear husband Jeff for graciously allowing me to work endless hours on this project. He has been continually supportive and patient while I have been in "writing zone-out mode." No more cheese and crackers for dinner, honey! I'm back on the home front again.

At least for a while....

Made in the USA
Middletown, DE
17 July 2016